The Bible and the Qur'an

A Question of Integrity

The Bible and the Qur'an

A Question of Integrity

Steven Masood

OM
publishing

The Bible and the Qur'an first published in 2001
by OM Publishing
Reprinted 2002 by Authentic Lifestyle

07 06 05 04 03 02   7 6 5 4 3 2

Authentic Lifestyle is an imprint of Authentic Media.
PO Box 300, Carlisle, Cumbria, CA3 0QS, UK
and PO Box 1047, Waynesboro, GA 30830-2047, USA
www.paternoster-publishing.com

British Library Cataloguing in Publication Data

A catalogue for this book is available from the British Library

ISBN 1-85078-369-1

Cover design by Philip Ronson
Typeset by WestKey Ltd, Falmouth, Cornwall
Printed in Denmark by Nørhaven Paperback A/S

To both Muslims and Christians

Contents

List of illustrations

Preface and acknowledgements

Dedicated to Muslims and Christians who wish to come closer to each other; to those who are struggling for religious and spiritual survival in an ever more quickly changing world, and also to those who would like to be more at home with the sacred in us all.

With appreciation and thanks to all my friends, both Muslims and Christians; to my fellow students and colleagues who kindly lent me books or made helpful suggestions on various matters; to Cynthia Lees and Peter Sinclair for their extra efforts to find books and works of reference.

My special thanks also to Asghar Ali, Anne Cooper, Zafar Ismail, Paul and Joanne Monk, Adel El Naggar, Philip Ronson, Keith Small, Vivienne Stacey, Kenneth Stocks, and Sally Sutcliffe, not just for their thoughtful contributions, but also for all their enlightening conversations and valuable help with sources. I am grateful to the editors at Paternoster for their unfailing co-operation and efficiency. However, none of them bears any responsibility for any of the ideas expressed and material presented in this book.

Qur'anic quotations are adapted from Yusuf Ali's *The Holy Qur'an: Text, Translation and Commentary* (Maryland: Amana Corporation, 1983), and *HOLY QUR'AN with*

English Translation by Muhammad Marmaduke Pickthall, (New Delhi: Kitab Bhavan, 1992).

Transliteration of Qur'anic words in Arabic follow Haleem Eliasii's, *The Holy Qur-'aan: Transliteration in Roman Script*, (Delhi: Faheem Publishers, 1981).

All dates are CE (Christian era) unless otherwise stated as BCE (Before the Christian era).

Introduction

Islam and Christianity claim to be **revealed** and **historical** faiths. They both claim that God intervened in the lives of people to lead them into 'the straight path'. Both set great store by the records they hold. The truth of their faith is held to depend on the accuracy of their books and traditions. When the believers of these two faiths, Muslims and Christians, read each other's Scriptures, they find many similarities but also some important differences.

Muslims believe that the original messages transmitted by previous prophets including Moses and Jesus, were essentially the same as the message brought by Muhammad and preserved in the Qur'an. They conclude that the differences arise from errors in the Bible; the divergence must be the result of some problem with the Bible alone. It is not the Qur'an, they assert, but the Bible that is in the wrong. They claim that Christians and Jews have added their own innovations to the Bible during the course of time, so there are bound to be differences between the teachings of the two Scriptures.

Against such views Christians believe that the Bible's message has not been corrupted, and that the differences between the Bible and the Qur'an are due to the circumstances of the production of the Qur'an, and *not* to changes in the Bible. For Christians the Bible is a reliable record of God's revelations. Since they claim the trustworthiness of the Bible, they question the Muslim claims for the Qur'an.

These conflicting views cause us to question the **authenticity** and **integrity** of both Scriptures. Certainly, a minority of Muslims do believe in the integrity of the Bible but it is the majority opinion which concerns us: that the Bible is corrupted in such a way that it cannot be trusted while the Qur'an is perfect, intact, word for word, syllable for syllable, as it was first revealed to Muhammad.

Since the rise of higher biblical criticism in the wake of the 17th–18th century Enlightenment, Muslims have also adopted the methods of Western critics, using their sophisticated tools to discredit the Bible. However, they do not dare to apply the same instruments and techniques of **biblical criticism** to the Qur'an and other Islamic sources. Those few who have published thoughtful but inconsequential speculation have found themselves condemned in *fatwah*, decrees declaring them to be apostates and beyond the pale of Islam. Thus the many who are fearful of violent repercussions tend to steer clear and confine themselves to applying the new methods of interpretation to the exegesis of the text, while the more fundamental questions on the validity and sources of the text of the Qur'an remain unasked.

The theory of **corruption**, as used to discredit the Bible, is not restricted to a few academics or adults: from the age of six or seven, Muslim children are also taught that corruption has occurred. For example, the following passage is from a book written for children and used in many Islamic centres in the United Kingdom.

The Qur'an has in it the names of the other books which were sent down by Allah to earlier messengers before Muhammad (pbuh). The book given to the prophet Ibrahim (pbuh) is called SAHIFA (scrolls). The prophet Musa (pbuh) was given TAWRAT (Torah). The prophet Dawud (pbuh) was given ZABUR (Psalms). The prophet Isa (pbuh) was given INJIL (Gospel). Books given to the prophets before Muhammad (pbuh) were either lost or changed by their followers.

The Sahifa of Ibrahim (pbuh) cannot be found now. The Zabur, the Tawrat and the Injil have been changed by their followers. They added their own words. This is why we do not get these books as they came in first. The Qur'an is the complete book of guidance from Allah, it is with us today, without any change, with nothing added or taken away. It is the last book of guidance for mankind from Allah.[1]

Another book written for children adds the idea that 'A Muslim believes in all the Books of Allah. But as the earliest Books are lost or changed, a Muslim follows the Qur'an alone.'[2]

Whether Muslim or Christian, no one likes having their holy books criticised. However, if a book is held up as perfect, as having fully preserved the message of God, then its perfection should be demonstrable against all criticism and tests of its contents. The standards and measures chosen should be equally applicable to any book which calls itself inspired, which would appear to include the Bible and the Qur'an.

It is with this desire that the following pages are put together. In them, we will look at the **standards** for scriptural integrity set up by Muslims and Christians in their conversations and writings, and to apply these same standards to both the Bible and the Qur'an. Islamic, Christian and other sources are used to shed light on various related issues. While some examples are dealt with in detail, this

---

[1] Ghulam Sarwar, *Islam for Younger people*, p.29.

[2] *The Children's Book of Islam*, part 1; p.22.

brief book cannot be an exhaustive study. The intention is to rather concentrate on the essential issues, typical questions, and problems raised between Muslims and Christians. It hopes to show how some arguments can lead to serious errors if they are used as a 'standard' with which to check the authority of a Scripture.

The first three chapters detail the **ideologies** which have grown up around Muslim and Christian beliefs, and theories of how the Scriptures are inspired and preserved. Both the **traditions** and the **historicity** of the Bible and the Qur'an are presented and compared. Chapter 4 surveys and challenges the Qur'anic testimony that no one can change the Word of God. In Chapter 5 the discussion targets the question of **errors and contradictions** within the texts of the Bible and the Qur'an. Chapter 6 addresses the argument that the Qur'an does not confirm the Scriptures which Christians have today. Statements like the following are dealt with: 'The Bible is unknown to the Qur'an; there was only one Injil (New Testament) and, because Christians do not have the Gospel in the Aramaic in which it was first written, the current gospel narratives are untrustworthy.' Some light is also thrown on subjects like *Isnad* the chain of transmission, pagan origins and the human element in the Bible and the Qur'an.

Some people claim that a document named **The Gospel of Barnabas** is the original Gospel. Some even base their presentation of the life and teaching of Jesus upon this document, rather than on the Qur'an, the Bible or the traditions. Chapter 7 addresses this issue.

The majority of Muslims affirm their faith in the miraculous nature of the Qur'an, *Ijaz al-Qur'an*. They believe that because of its divine origin, no text 'like' the Qur'an could be produced. Some Muslims reject the Bible because they believe its teaching and content is not as clear and eloquent as the text of the Qur'an. Chapter 8 goes into detail on this subject, considering the side effects which such a belief in **inimitability** brings. Chapter 9 deals with the Islamic doctrine of **abrogation,** *al-Naskh wa al-Mansukh,* to enquire whether it is the Bible or only parts of the Qur'anic revelation that are annulled. Finally, Chapter 10 brings all these themes together to conclude the whole discussion.

1

The Scriptures: the traditional views

Muslims and Christians believe that God chose to reveal himself and his will to people by speaking through prophets and apostles. He enabled them to share his message with their fellow human beings in order to explain our existence on earth and our direction for the future. Christians believe that the Bible contains the necessary guidance while Muslims uphold the Qur'an and value its direction.

The Bible

The title 'Bible' is derived from a Greek word, *biblia*, originating in *biblos* and is a translation of the Hebrew word *seper*; the term simply means 'books'.[1] It is suggested that the title was used by early Christians. The earliest evidence for the use of this title by Christians is found in the second letter of Clement (d.150).[2] As a title, it appears in the lists of the canonical books in the 5th century. It was adopted into Latin and came into English as *bibul*, *bibil* and, at last, with the modern spelling of 'Bible'.

---

[1] Colin Brown (ed.), *New International Dictionary of New Testament Theology*, Vol.1. pp.242–244.

[2] Derek Williams (ed.), *New Concise Bible Dictionary*, p.60.

There are two main sections of the Bible: the Old Testament and the New Testament. The word 'Testament' is from the Latin word *testamentum*, which is used to translate the Greek word *diatheke* (covenant), thereby denoting the relationship between God and his people (cf. 2 Corinthians 3:6, 14; Hebrews 9:15). In Arabic, words like *Misaq* or *Ahd* stand for 'covenant'. Thus in the Arabic, Urdu and Farsi languages, the Old and New Testament are called 'Ahd al-Qadim' and 'Ahd al-Jadid'.

It is possible to divide the Bible into four major parts: the Torah, the Psalms, the books of the Prophets and the *Injil*, the Gospel. The word *Injil* here is taken in its broadest sense to mean the whole of the New Testament. The Bible contains law, prophecy, history, poetry, counsel and much more. The contents of the Old Testament section of the Bible, which the Jews also accept as their holy book in its entirety, were written centuries before Christ, mainly in the Hebrew language. However, they do not call it the Old Testament. Rather it is referred to as the *TeNaKh*, an acronym based on the initial letters of the three words *Torah*, law, *Nebi'im*, prophets, and *Ketubim*, writings.[3] The books of the New Testament were written in Greek, which was the common language in use at the time, much as English is in some way the universal language today. However, as time passed, translations were made into other languages for people from other nationalities, backgrounds and languages.

Most Christians see the Bible as containing insights into God's dealings with the people of Israel. These dealings eventually paved the way for all the peoples of the earth to share in the promise that God first made to Abraham, (who is known to Muslims as Ibrahim). Christians believe that God fulfilled this promise by sending Jesus. Furthermore, they assert that the Bible tells them, in more detail

[3] F. F. Bruce, *The Canon of Scripture*, pp.19, 29.

than any other book, who Jesus was and how he fulfilled
the ancient prophecies about him, as given through Abraham, Moses and other prophets. Although for Christians
the Bible is significant, it is Jesus who is the eternal Word
and the Revelation of God, and the Bible is the written
record or Scripture which unfolds the story of salvation
for all human beings, as achieved through Jesus.

The Qur'an

The title comes from a verb *qara'a* which means to recite.[4]
In early Kufic manuscripts the word *Qur'an* was written
without a diacritic or vowel point known as *hamza*, which
caused some to believe that the word *Qur'an* was from
Qarna, to put together.[5] Other scholars such as oriental-
ists, believe that the word Qur'an may be derived from the
Syriac word *qeryana*, meaning 'Scripture reading, lesson';
the word *qeryana* was used in Christian liturgy in the 5th to
7th century liturgical phrase, *qeryana d-yom ba'awatta*,
meaning 'readings for the day of supplication'.[6]

The Qur'an comprises 114 chapters. Each chapter is
called a *surah* (pl. *suwar*). The corresponding word in
Hebrew *shurah* means a row, e.g. of bricks in a wall.[7] Each
surah is divided into verses, termed *ayat*, (sing. *aya* or
ayah), a word which is related to the Hebrew *oth* and Syriac
atha.[8] There are different systems of numbering the verses.

[4] Subhi Salih, *Ulum al-Qur'an*, p.25.
[5] Jalaluddin Suyuti, *Al-Itqan fi Ulum al-Qur'an*, Vol 1. pp.117, 135.
[6] *The Encyclopaedia of Islam*, Vol.5, p.400.
[7] Muhammad Abdulla Pasha, *Sixth Century and Beyond*, p.75. See also: Arthur Jeffery, *Foreign Vocabulary of the Qur'an*, pp.180–182.
[8] Arthur Jeffery, *Foreign Vocabulary of the Qur'an*, pp.72–73.

According to *Koofi* there are 6239 verses in the Qur'an; the *Shami* system makes it 6225; the *Makki* system declares 6219; according to *Madni* they number 6211, but according to the *Basri* system, the verses total 6204.[9] However, most Muslim writers state that the number of verses in the Qur'an is 6247 or 6360 if the opening verse of *Bismillah* for each *surah* is included. Each *surah* is traditionally labelled as Makkan (revealed in Makkah) or Madinan (revealed in Madina). Makkan revelations are in some places inter-mixed with Madinan revelations, so a *surah* marked as Makkan may also contain verses revealed to Muhammad during the Madinan period, and vice versa. The collection of *suwah* in the Qur'an as we have it today shows no chrono-logical order of composition, although many scholars both Muslims and non-Muslims have tried to construct one.

To Muslims, the Qur'an is the word of God 'vowel for vowel, syllable for syllable'[10], revealed in Arabic to Muhammad through the angel Gabriel at intervals over a period of some twenty years. It is considered to be uncreated and eternally existent on *lauh mahfuz*, a guarded tablet in heaven (Surah 85:22). Though the Qur'an was sent to Muhammad at specific times, it was always there with God. As God is, the Qur'an is.

The Qur'an describes itself in several passages as being the word of God. It is from Allah, the God of Ibrahim, Ismael, Ishaq, Yaqub and Musa, the same God who revealed the Torah and the Injil. It deals with three main themes: *Tawhid*, the unity of God, *Risalh*, the prophethood and *Akhira*, the hereafter. The message for the most part is plain and direct, though some passages are acknowl-edged to be obscure. The traditional belief of many Mus-lims is that the Qur'an cannot be fully expressed in other

[9] Qamar Naqvi, *Sahayef*, p.395.
[10] Abul A'ala Mawdudi, *The Message of the Prophet's Seerat*, p.14.

languages than Arabic. Translations are available, however, as produced by both Muslims and non-Muslims. As with the Bible, both classical and modern commentaries are also available which differ, sometimes radically, in their interpretations of the text.

The Islamic and Christian views of revelation

The subject of revelation is important to both Muslims and Christians. The Arabic verb and noun, *awha* and *wahy* are the technical terms of Islamic theology for the communication of the messages or revelations to Muhammad. They occur more than sixty times in the Qur'an and are usually translated into English as 'revelation' or 'inspiration'. Another word, *nazzala*, sent down, is also used in the Qur'an as the equivalent of *awha*. 'It is He who sent down to thee the Book', *nazzala alaykal-Kitaaba* (Surah 3:3).

The Qur'an speaks of the various ways by which the revelation was sent, but more can be found about its forms and methods in the *Ahadith*, the collections of traditions. The traditional views were developed in the second and the third centuries of Islam, and emphasise that revelation came in different forms.[11] Sometimes a revelation was a sudden introduction of an idea into the mind. Some revelations were through dreams and visions. At other times God spoke directly. However, often he sent his angel to deliver the message either in person or indirectly.[12] The traditional belief is that there was no human contribution to the process. God's word was conveyed verbatim to Muhammad. He simply heard it and faithfully conveyed it to his companions who preserved it in their memory, and some wrote it down as well.

---

[11] Fazlur Rahman, *Islam*, p.31.
[12] Muhammad Abdulla Pasha, *Sixth Century and Beyond*, p.39.

Syed Hossein Nassr claims, 'No Muslim would accept any other view than the Qur'an came verbatim from heaven.'[13] Another Muslim scholar, Fazlur Rahman, however believes that, 'the Qur'an is entirely the Word of God and, in an ordinary sense, also entirely the Word of Muhammad'.[14] Taking this a step further, Ali Dashti gives several examples from the Qur'an, asserting that it also contains statements from Muhammad on God's behalf.[15]

Explaining the process of revelation, Muslim scholars claim that Muhammad's experience of receiving revelation was a different kind of consciousness: perspiration would pour from his forehead; occasionally he would snort like a camel or be taken by a seizure; often his eyes would turn red. At times Gabriel would bring revelation appearing in the form of a handsome young man or in his own form, with six hundred wings, each of which blocked the horizon. At other times, no person or being would be visible but the revelation came to Muhammad with a noise resembling the sound of bells.[16] Muslim sources also relate that at times Muhammad was uncertain of his revelation.

Circumstances were not always right for the revelation to descend. Once a puppy entered his house and died under the bedstead. Gabriel did not come until after the dead body was removed and the place cleansed. Al-Bukhari (d.870) and Al-Suyuti (d.1500) record that Gabriel would not enter a house where there was a dog or a picture.[17]

---

[13] Syed Hossein Nassr, 'Responses to Hans Kung's paper on Christian Muslim Dialogue', Muslim World, 77, 1987. p.98.

[14] Fazlur Rahman, Islam, p.31.

[15] Ali Dashti, Twenty-three years, p.149.

[16] Sahih al-Bukhari, Vol 1, p.2.

[17] Suyuti, Al-Itqan fi Ulum al-Qur'an, Vol. 1, p.81.

Influenced by these beliefs, many Muslims think that the Scriptures of both Jews and Christians should have descended in the same manner as is claimed for the Qur'an. However, some Muslims do differentiate between the Qur'an and earlier Scriptures in their manner of 'descending' on prophets and apostles. Ibn Khaldun (d.1406), a great Muslim historian, while holding to the orthodox idea about the Qur'an having descended word for word on Muhammad, claims that the Qur'an 'differs from the Torah, the Gospel and other heavenly books. The prophets received their books in the form of ideas during the state of revelation. After their return to a human state, they expressed those ideas in their own ordinary words.'[18]

Although a Muslim, Ibn Khaldun seems to have come close to the Christian understanding of the way inspiration operated in the receipt of their own Scriptures. However, the Bible does not mention the prophets fainting or feeling heavy during the receiving of revelation. The way these prophets and apostles received God's word is very different from the popular Muslim understanding. Their experiences of revelation were not physically painful or oppressive. By studying the text of the Bible, it becomes obvious that the recipients were enabled to distinguish divine truth. Even in the case of Christ's disciples, they were given the assurance, 'it will not be you speaking, but the Spirit of your Father speaking through you.' (Matthew 10:20). In another place Jesus said to them, 'I will give you words and wisdom that none of your adversaries will be able to resist or contradict' (Luke 21:15).

Christians believe what the Bible says, 'In the past God spoke to our fathers through the prophets at many times and in various ways' (Hebrews 1:1). There was a gradual unfolding of the revelation. The Bible declares that God used many methods to reveal his word and purpose. To

---

[18] Ibn Khaldun, *The Muqaddimah*, p.74.

some he spoke directly, while to others he spoke in dreams or visions. To yet others he sent angels. He used their normal intelligence and their own literary style of writing. Christians claim that the Holy Spirit[19] of God is responsible for the revelation. The recipients 'spoke from God as they were carried along by the Holy Spirit' (2 Peter 1:21; 1 Thessalonians 2:13). They believe that their 'Scripture is God-breathed and is useful for teaching, rebuking, correcting and training in righteousness, so that the man of God may be thoroughly equipped for every good work' (2 Timothy 3:16–17).

So Christians speak of the writers of the books of the Bible, not so much as having 'received revelations' by ecstasy or by word-for-word dictation,[20] but as being 'inspired', *theopneustos* or in the original Greek meaning, 'God-breathed'. In other words they were guided by God's spirit as they wrote (and spoke on occasions). They were not always passive receivers of a 'word for word' document.

Another point to consider is that the Bible is not something received through one person, nor was it produced during a relatively short period of time as was the Qur'an. Some forty individuals, including kings, shepherds, fishermen, civil servants, priests, at least one general and a physician, were involved in the writing of this collection. Although they wrote and put the words together at different times and in different circumstances, there is, however, a remarkable uniformity in their central themes: the salvation of people.

In the Bible, some of the recipients of revelations have used expressions like, 'The Spirit of the Lord spoke to me',

---

[19] Muslims believe that the Holy Spirit is the angel Gabriel but Christians reject such a notion; they believe that the Holy Spirit is divine.

[20] Carson and Woodbridge (eds.), *Scripture and Truth*, p.205.

'This is what the Lord says' or 'The word of the Lord came to me'. In some places, we find experiences like that of the prophet Jeremiah, who said, 'Then the Lord reached out his hand and touched my mouth and said to me, "Now I have put my words in your mouth . . ." ' (Jeremiah 1:9).

God's revelation in action

The Bible begins with a simple outline of the story of creation and records the main events in Adam's life (Genesis 2–4). It then moves on to the story of Noah and Abraham's encounters with God (Genesis 5–25). Condensed versions of these accounts can also be found in the Qur'an. Then there is the story of Isaac, Ishmael, Jacob (also called Israel) and his descendants (known as Bani Israel, the Children of Israel). Their story is one of the colourful and memorable phases of Old Testament history (Genesis 25–36). The link between the patriarchs and the arrival of a recognisable people of Israel is provided by the story of Joseph (Genesis 37–50), celebrated in retellings in the Qur'an (Surah 12).

During the time of Moses, the climax of God's revelation was the deliverance of the Israelites from Egypt and the giving of the Law (Exodus 1–40). These events are also mentioned in the Qur'an (Surah 2:51–53; 3:3; 7:103–157, etc.). Based on the oral narrative of these events, the Torah became the accepted written account of God's Law to the Israelites and also an account of how God redeemed his distressed people at particular times and places in history. God continued this process of intervening in human history. Thus many books of the Bible contain the narratives, commands and histories of the prophets. For example, the books of the prophets, the Psalms and Chronicles contain the materials that make up the remainder of the Old Testament after the Torah.

Christians state that God's revelation reached its climax around 2,000 years ago in the person of Jesus, the Christ. Both Muslims and Christians describe Jesus as the Word of God, although they may disagree in their understanding of this title. Jesus accepted the integrity of the Old Testament books. In his teaching and preaching, he referred to them as Scriptures (John 5:39; Matthew 21:42; 22:29; 26:54; Luke 4:21; 24:27; Mark 12:10). It is on his authority that Christians accept the validity of the Old Testament.

As for the New Testament, Christians do not believe that it descended on Jesus in the way the Qur'an is said to have descended on Muhammad. For them Jesus, as the Word of God, is God's revelation in action (John 1:1–14; Revelation 19:13; Hebrews 1:2). Jesus not only preached the gospel, the good news of reconciliation of people to God; his life, death and resurrection were also an essential part of that redemption process. Following Jesus' command, the disciples passed on this good news to the following generations, as preserved in the written accounts we now call the New Testament section of the Bible.

So in Islam, the Qur'an as the Word of God has a primary status while Muhammad has the secondary status. In contrast, in Christianity it is Jesus who has the primary status as the Word of God and the Bible has a secondary status. According to Islamic theology, the Word of God became a book; according to Christology God spoke and sent his message to the world through various people, but finally sent Jesus as his Word. Hence, while Muslims refer to the Qur'an, a book, as divine and eternal, Christians refer to Jesus as divine and eternal, thereby emphasising that Jesus was with God before time began.

The aim of the revelation

The need to *surrender to God's will* has always been central to God's message, and we see good examples of it in the lives of his people. For example, Abraham surrendered himself and obeyed God's call to migrate to a foreign land. It was because of his faith in God and obedience in submission to God and his righteousness that he was called *Khalil ul-llah*, the friend of God (Qur'an, Surah 4:125; Bible, James 2:23). Moses, who could have lived an easy life, refused to remain in luxury as a member of Pharaoh's family. He surrendered himself to God and led the Israelites to freedom, out of their bondage to Egypt (Qur'an, Surah 7:103 ff.; 26:18 ff.; Bible, Hebrews 11:24).

Jesus in the garden of Gethsemane, prayed, 'not my will, but yours be done.' (Luke 22:42). There is no disagreement between Christians and Muslims on the subject of surrendering to God. They even share the belief that 'In the past God spoke to our forefathers through the prophets at many times and in various ways' (Hebrews 1:1). There is disagreement, however, when considering whether God actually concluded his message by speaking through Jesus. Muslims claim that the mission of Jesus was not a universal one; he was sent only to the Israelites. It is the prophet Muhammad, they believe, who was sent for *all* people about six hundred years after Jesus.

The traditional view of the compilation of the Scriptures

It is uncertain when the whole of the Old Testament was first compiled to form a 'canon'. It is known, however, that at least three hundred years before Jesus, the books of the Torah, the Psalms and the prophets were not only available together, but were also translated into a Greek version known as the *Septuagint*. Jesus in his teaching referred to and quoted from many parts of these Scriptures asserting that, 'These are the Scriptures that testify about me . . .' (John 5:39). For this reason the Jewish Scriptures gained an enormous importance in Christian history, being regarded as a major part of their holy Scriptures.

The books of the New Testament were put together after Jesus' ascension. The epistles were written between 49–70 CE with the exception of the epistles of John and the Revelation, which were written in 80–100. The majority of New Testament scholars agree on the following dates for the four Gospels which are the main part of the New Testament: Matthew, 50–70; Mark, 65–70; Luke, 60–70 and John at around the end of the first century. There are scholars, however, who claim that all of the New Testament was available in written form before 70 CE.[21]

Although it is part and parcel of Islamic belief to believe in the Scriptures of Christians and Jews, the majority of Muslims do not accept what Christians and Jews read today as Scriptures. For example, they do not accept the New Testament as being *'the'* Gospel. In their view, Jesus received a revelation called 'Injil', which they assume he must have passed verbatim to his disciples.

Many Muslims believe that Jesus was given something that was written because they read in the Qur'an that Jesus was 'given the gospel' (Surah 5:46; 57:27) and that he 'was given the Scripture' (Surah 19:30). The fact is that neither Jesus, nor Muhammad, nor any other prophet received anything in writing from God. The sole exception is Moses, who only received the ten commandments in writing; the rest of the law was given to him through other means. The Qur'an does say that God sent (*anzala*) the

---

[21] Robinson, *Redating the New Testament*, p.221–53.

Gospel, and that Jesus was given (*a'tenaho*) 'the book', although it may not be literally a book or books that he received. Neither does the Qur'an indicate that Jesus received revelation in the same way as Muhammad did. In other places the Qur'an says that Jesus was taught the book, the Torah and the Injil (Surah 5:110). This does not mean that he became the recipient of the Gospel, in the same way as Muhammad received the Qur'an.

Neither the Gospel narratives in the New Testament, nor history offer any evidence for the Muslim belief that Jesus received a book from heaven which he then passed on to his disciples. Instead the Gospel narratives record Jesus' promise to send the Holy Spirit who would remind them what he had said (John 14:26; 16:13). It was with this guidance that the disciples wrote what Christians now have as the New Testament. The disciples were persuaded to do so because Jesus instructed them to declare openly what had been revealed to them and what he had said to them (Matthew 10:26f). No wonder the apostolic writings, that is the epistles in the New Testament, are also called the 'word of God' just as much as the word of Jesus is (cf. Luke 5:1; 8:21 with 1 Corinthians 14:26; Colossians. 1:25). The result of this understanding was that early Christianity accepted both the words of Jesus, as transmitted in the Gospels and the apostolic writings, and gave them recognition as authoritative records of the divine revelation. It is noteworthy that the Qur'an also testifies that the apostles of Jesus were inspired by God (Surah 5:111).

So what then is the gospel, the Injil, which Jesus mentioned? Christians claim that this word refers to the 'good news'. It was used by Jesus, his apostles and disciples not as the title of a book, but a description of a message, the good news about Jesus and his redeeming love.

In contrast with the views of Christians, Muslims believe that the Qur'an was revealed in stages during the lifetime of Muhammad. Only Muhammad received the revelation, which he then dictated to his companions. It was memorised by him and his companions. Most of it was also written down on whatever material was available.[22] Among those who wrote such fragments were Uthman bin Affan, Ali bin Abi Talib, Muawiyya bin Abi Sufyan, Abdullah bin Masood, Ubayy Ibn Kab, Zaid Ibn Thabit and Abd Allah Ibn Abi Sara and several others. It is said that Muhammad instructed scribes where to place newly revealed passages.

Recension of the Qur'an and the Bible

We learn from Islamic sources that by the time of Muhammad's death, there was no complete official copy of the Qur'an available. The companions who were recommended by Muhammad as teachers of the Qur'an found that each had a collection of material that was different in terms of the numbers of chapters and in the actual text itself. According to popular traditions, the first attempt to compile these fragments into one volume (the process of recension) took place during the reign of the first caliph, Abu Bakr (632–634 CE), but it was during the time of Uthman (644–656), the third caliph, that a standard 'official' copy of the Qur'an was first prepared. This version was written in unpointed consonantal script. All other collections were ordered to be burnt (See Chapter 2 for details). At the time of the Ummayad caliph, Abd al-Malik (685–705), the formal introduction of diacritical marks and vowel points had begun. However, the available manuscripts show that such work along with some other crucial refinements continued well into the fourth and

---

[22] Ahmad von Denffer, *Ulum al-Qur'an*, p.37.

fifth century of Islam.[23] In spite of such a history, Muslims believe that today's copies are directly descended from the time of Uthman with the diacritical marks from the time of Al Hajjaj ibn Yusuf (d.714), the governor general of Iraq under Abd al-Malik. It is also part of Muslims' belief that since God himself promised to be the protector of the Qur'an, it has indeed been preserved, word for word, as it was revealed to the Prophet Muhammad.

When we look at the history of the recension of the Bible we find, in contrast with the Qur'an, that Jews and Christians never attempted an 'official' compilation of their books. In part, this was because they were not in a position of political power as Muslims were. Several centuries before Christ, the majority of the Jews agreed on the 39 books of the Bible which are available today in the Old Testament. At the Jewish council of Jamnia held in 90 CE, the same 39 books were recognised as Holy Scripture. Following Christ's example, Christians accepted them as well. Naturally there have been debates about the books of the Old Testament just as there were among the early generations of Muslims about some parts of the Qur'an.

As for the New Testament, the four gospels Matthew, Mark, Luke and John, along with the 13 epistles of Paul, were known to have been written by or under the authority of the apostles of Jesus. However, the earliest list which corresponds to the New Testament as we have it today stems from Athanasius in his Easter Letter of the year 367.[24] The first major council of the Church to list the 27 books of the New Testament was the Synod of Hippo in the year 393. Christians believe that while such Church councils did not *confer* canonicity or demark the canon by an arbitrary decree, they did recognise and ratify the

---

[23] Welch, 'Al-KUR'AN' in *The Encyclopaedia of Islam*, Vol. 5, p.408; see also Abbott, *Rise of the North Arabic Script*, pp.17–44.

[24] F. F. Bruce, *The Books and the Parchments*, p.112.

widespread consensus (*ijma*), that had already developed concerning the boundaries of the New Testament.

Conclusion

Although Muslims and Christians differ on the modes of revelation and inspiration, both sides uphold the view that their Scriptures are inspired and have been preserved very well through the ages. They both believe in the integrity of their Scriptures. Christians believe that the Bible is the true record of God's message and his dealings. It is the Bible, they believe, that reveals how people can return to God. Conversely, Muslims believe that God revealed the concluding part of his message through Muhammad. Christians believe that Jesus not only came with the final messages of God, but that he himself was the revelation of the nature of God.

We find Christians wholeheartedly admitting that God allowed a human element to come through in both the writing and the transmission of their Scriptures, but Muslims take such an admission to be evidence and proof of the Bible's unreliability. They believe that the Qur'an is reliable because it is preserved letter for letter as it was revealed to Muhammad and that there was no human element in the transmission and recension to interfere with the text of the Qur'an, a claim we will return to.

2

Evidence of reliability (1)

It is important to know what evidence exists when considering the reliability of the texts of the Bible and Qur'an.
The texts of these two books did not come into being all at
once, so one has to find out what processes of redaction
and 'final adjustment' took place. From the history of the
transmission and recension of the Qur'an and the Bible,
we find that both Scriptures were put together over particular periods of time, the Bible between 1,450 BCE and 100
CE and the Qur'an 610–650 CE. What evidence is available
to verify their integrity, veracity and reliability? To find
answers, we will consider the evidence of some of the
available manuscripts, related documents, and other discoveries. This study is important because there are so
many Muslims who believe that the Bible has not been
preserved in such a way that it can be trusted, yet believe
the Qur'an *is* well preserved and is therefore beyond such
criticism.

   Academics call an original manuscript an 'autograph'.
There are no autographs of any part of the Bible or of the
Qur'an. The same is true in fact of all classical writings of
antiquity. However, there are early copies of manuscripts
available to us. There are also other documents available
to check what Muslims and Christians believe about their
respective Scriptures. In this chapter, we will look at the

case of the Qur'an. We will follow it in the next chapter with the evidence for the reliability of the Bible.

The text of the Qur'an

Manuscript copies of the Qur'an from the century that it was compiled are not available. While some writers say that a number of odd fragments are from the first century of the Islamic calendar, it can be safely stated as in Ahmad von Denffers' words, 'Most of the early original Qur'an manuscripts, complete or in sizeable fragments, that are still available to us now, are not earlier than the second century after the Hijrah.'[1] In spite of the continuous political supremacy of an Islamic empire, ruling over communities with a highly developed literary tradition, where Arabic became the essential language of religion, politics and commerce, significant first century Qur'anic manuscripts do not exist. Similarly, there are no manuscripts at hand relating to the Islamic community during the period between the first Arab conquest (early 7th century CE) and the appearance, with the *Sira-Maghazi* narratives, of the earliest Islamic literature in the late 8th century CE.

Muslims often state that two of the *Uthmanic* recension copies from the time of caliph Uthman (cir. 650) are still available. One is said to be the copy preserved in the state library at Tashkent in Uzbekistan, known as the *Samarkand* or *Tashkent* codex.[2] It is written on parchment. About half of this manuscript has survived. It begins with the seventh verse of Surah 2 of the Qur'an and finishes with the text from Surah 43, verse 10. This means that 72 of the 114 known chapters of the Qur'an in this manuscript

---

[1] Ahmad von Denffer, *Ulum Al-Qur'an*, pp.60–61.

[2] Muslim authorities have not allowed serious textual criticism and other processes to date these manuscripts

Figure 1. Verse from the Samarkand Kufic Qur'an
Top: *A page from the Qur'an said to be one of the 'Uthmanic' copies
sent out to various provinces. The text is in Kufic script without linear
uniformity. The copyist left out several words in the middle of the
second line; these were later added in the margin. It is also possible that
these words were added to correct the different Uthmanic versions.*
Bottom: *Today's version of the same passage (Surah 6:146) which has
incorporated the words in the margin into the main text.*

are missing entirely. In addition there are many intervening pages missing. It is written in a particular Kufic script
which, according to modern experts in Arabic calligraphy,
did not exist until late in the eighth century CE and was
not in use at all in Makkah and Madinah in the seventh
century.[3] Although Muslim writers treat the document as
coming from 650 CE,[4] Western orthographers,

---

[3] Lings and Safadi, *The Qur'an*, pp. 12,13,17.
[4] *History of the Mushaf of Uthman in Tashkent*, cited by Ahmad von
Denffer, *Ulum Al-Qur'an*, p.64.

Figure 2. The Topkapi codex
A page from the Topkapi codex in Istanbul . Although it is claimed to be
an 'Uthmanic' copy, it differs in many details from the Samarkand
copy and also has more lines per page. The manuscript cannot date
earlier than the late eight century CE.

scriptologists and other researchers believe that the textual style of calligraphy and the artistic illuminations
between the chapters are characteristic of a period at least
one hundred and fifty years after Muhammad's death.[5]
This means it cannot be either the copy prepared by
Uthman for that region or the one that he was reading
when assassinated in 656.

The other manuscript is the 'Topkapi' codex housed in
the Topkapi Museum in Istanbul, Turkey. It is also written
in a Kufic script on parchment with similar ornaments
between chapters. However a comparison between the

---

[5] Isaac Mendelsohn, 'The Samarqand Kufic Qur'an', *Muslim
World*, **30**, 1940, p.378.

two codices shows that they were not transcribed in the same place or at the same time. One difference is that while the Topkapi codex has eighteen lines to the page, the Samarkand has between eight and twelve.

For both copies of the Qur'an, an analysis of the style and calligraphy suggests that they are indeed the oldest manuscripts of the Qur'an available but that they cannot be dated earlier than the second century of Islam, almost one and a half centuries after the Uthman recension.[6]

There are a few other manuscripts, some of which are in private collections. The copies that are openly available for study are all from a later time than those above. In later centuries of Islam, the calligraphers' names used to appear, usually at the end of the text of the Qur'an together with the date and place where the codex was copied, a device known as a colophon. However researchers have found that some of the colophons in these manuscripts are known to have been forged and thus the dating and identification in that form becomes unreliable.

Among other manuscripts of the Qur'an available today and housed in the National Library of Tunisia is one which was originally inscribed in the late ninth century or early tenth century. The script *Mashq* is employed. It is suggested that this copy was not meant for general reading and was written for the Abbasid Caliph, al-Mamun, for the tomb of his father, Harun ar-Rashid, at Mashhad in Persia. Somehow it did not make its way to him and remained in the land of its origin. Though a number of individual pages of it are held in private collections, the bulk of it is preserved in the library on display.

The oldest complete Qur'an, written in the *al-Mail* script, resides in the British Library, dated as from the end of the eighth century.[7] There are other surviving copies

---

[6] John Gilchrist, *The Qur'an: The Scriptures of Islam*, p.137.

[7] Lings and Safadi, *The Qur'an*, pp.17, 20.

Figure 3. The Qur'an in Al-Ma'il script

A page from one of the oldest copies of the Qur'an in al-Ma'il script, copied at Makka or Madina in the late 8th century CE. The passage is Surah 24:32–45 in the present Qur'an.

(Produced with permission of the British Library, Or 2165)

written at the same time in al-Mail or Hijazi script. There was one available in the National Library and Museum of Kuwait until the Iraqi invasion of 1990. Some believe it has been stolen by the Iraqi soldiers and carried away in their retreat.[8]

A manuscript of the Qur'an in the early Naskh script was written by the great Arab calligrapher Ibn al-Bawwab at Baghdad in 1001 CE. It now resides in the Chester Beatty Library in Dublin, Ireland.

Due to Muslim opposition, intermittent work continues on manuscripts found in Sana'a, Yemen, in 1972 and

---

[8] For a much fuller account: Gilchrist, *Jam'al-Qur'an*, (Benoni: *Jesus to Muslims*, 1989).

Figure 4. A page from a Qur'an manuscript

A double page from a Qur'an copy in al-Ma'il script written in the 8th century CE. The copy disappeared from the National Museum of Kuwait in the Gulf war of 1991.

housed in Yemen's House of Manuscripts. The oldest manuscript in the collection according to one scholar dates as early as 705 CE. It has some significant variations from the text of the Qur'an as used today. Whole sections are missing and, in some places, text has been added by much later hands.[9] According to Puin, a specialist in

---

[9] Research by Dr. Puin Gerd-Rudiger et al. of Saarland University, Saarbruken (published in German). Some Muslims are of the opinion that these manuscripts predate Uthman's official recension. These views were posted on the Internet in response to an article by Toby Lester, 'What is the Qur'an?' *The Atlantic Monthly*, January 1999; see also: The Guardian (England), Aug. 8,00; www.guardianunlimited.co.uk/education/story

Figure 5. The Ibn al-Bawwab Qur'an manuscript

The opening page showing the first Surah of the Qur'an and the start of the second Surah. It is said to have been written by the great calligrapher Ali Ibn Hilal known as Ibn al- Bawwab in 1001 CE. This is the oldest manuscript known in Naskh script.

(Picture produced with permission by Chester Beatty Library)

Arabic calligraphy and Qur'anic palaeography based at Saarland University, the Yemeni manuscripts seem to suggest 'an evolving text rather than simply the Word of God as revealed in its entirety'.[10] These studies allow us to conclude that until other discoveries are made, the earliest Qur'anic manuscripts available, apart from perhaps a few papyrus fragments and the incomplete San'a manuscript,

---

[10] Toby Lester, 'What is the Qur'an', *The Atlantic Monthly*, January 1999; see also: Puin, 'Observation on early Qur'an manuscripts' in San'a, pp. 107–11 in Stefan Wild's, 'The Qur'an as Text', (Leiden: Brill, 1996).

Figure 6. A page from the Yemeni Qur'an fragments
(Codex San'a 01–27.1)
The Script is of the Hijazi type and is part of Surah 20:1–10
(Picture by Dr Puin Gerd-Rudiger)

cannot be dated earlier than one hundred years after the time of Muhammad.

Available sources for the Qur'an

After Muhammad's death in 632, in a period of just one hundred years, Muslim conquests covered an area greater than the Roman Empire. Although internal and external conflicts continued, by the end of the 8th century, Islam started to crystallize as a religious and political entity. From this period onward a vast body of literature, historical and exegetical, evolved to explain the Islamic Scripture and its law. The most important elements of this era are the collections of the sayings and deeds of Muhammad known as *Hadith*, biographies of Muhammad (*Sirah*), and commentaries (*tafsir*) on the Qur'an. It is in these traditional sources that the documentary evidence for the history of the collection of the Qur'an and its content is most widely available.

Among the Hadith collections the compilation of Ismail al Bukhari (d.870) and that of Muslim ibn al-Hajjaj (d.875) are treated as the most authentic. Together, their collections are called *as-Sahihan*, the two authentics.[11] These collections are in fact part of a series known as *al-kutub as-sittah*. These sources represent the first-hand external authority concerning the reliability of the Qur'an in Muslim writings.

Some support is also found in the *Sirah* by Ibn Hisham (d.834) which is said to have been originally written by Ibn Ishaq (d.767). Other works like Ibn S'ad's (d.845) *Tabaqat* is of some value. It contains a long chapter devoted to an account of those who collected the Qur'an.

Most of the earliest commentators on the Qur'an relied on the Hadith and Sirah material. Later commentators added little and in fact, as time passed, many avoided any mention of either variant readings or the omission of texts in earlier copies of the Qur'an. A comprehensive assessment, based on all sources, reveals that the present collection of the Qur'an is far from being a complete and accurate copy of all that Muhammad taught his followers. The present Qur'an may contain the message of Muhammad but not the whole of it. Both Muslim and non-Muslim sources agree that the Qur'an has not come to us in full as was taught by Muhammad.

There could be many reasons for not having the whole of the Qur'an, but one is paramount. Muhammad did not give the whole of the Qur'an at one time nor did the

---

[11] Cyril Glasse, *The Concise Encyclopaedia of Islam*, p.342.

immediate circle of disciples commit all of it to writing.
Many Muslims were reciting portions of the Qur'an
which differed from each other. Though many Muslims
today think the differences were confined to pronunciation, a study of the sources shows that the differences were
more than that. It can be demonstrated from the various
traditions of Islam that the differences in the recitation of
the Qur'an extended far deeper than mere pronunciation,
and that there were differences in words, verses and even
chapters of the Qur'an. These differences existed even in
the days of Muhammad. For example, Abdullah reports:

> We differed about a Surah as to whether it consisted of thirty
> five or thirty six verses, so we went to the Prophet who was
> engaged in conversation with Ali. When we told him we dis-
> agreed over the reading, his face reddened as he replied,
> 'Those before you perished through their disagreements.' He
> whispered something to Ali who said, 'The Prophet com-
> mands you to recite as you were taught.'[12]

During Muhammad's lifetime, the Qur'an was not codi-
fied into an official compilation. Instead his companions
memorised different parts of the Qur'an and some were
written down piecemeal on all sorts of materials, palm-
leaves, stones, bones and leather, etc.[13] Had Muhammad
left a complete text with an official compilation, as some
Muslims claim that he did, there would have been no need
for his successors to have examined the various sources
after his death, and collected and compiled the text of the
Qur'an into one book.

---

[12] Tabari, Vol. 3, pp. 23–24, cited by John Burton, *The Collection of the Qur'an*, p.149.
[13] Suyuti, *Al-Itqan fi Ulum al-Qur'an*, Vol 1, p.96.

The compilation under Abu Bakr

According to *Sahih Bukhari*, the first compilation took place during the reign of the first caliph Abu Bakr (632–634). Shortly after Muhammad's death (d.632), several tribes from the outer regions of Arabia started a revolt and Abu Bakr had to send a large number of Muslims to suppress it. As a result of the ensuing battle of Yamama (633 CE), many of Muhammad's companions, who had memorised parts of the Qur'an, were killed. All this made Abu Bakr aware of the need to collect and preserve the Qur'an in *written* form.

According to Al-Qurtubi, 'During the Battle of Yamama, four hundred and fifty reciters of the Qur'an were killed.' In consequence, as Ibn Shihab relates, Abu Bakr was overwhelmed with sadness over such a loss. He adds: 'When Muslims in the Yamama combat were injured, Abu Bakr panicked. He was afraid that a portion of the Qur'an would be lost. Therefore people came with what they already had with them.'[14]

According to Al-Bukhari, Abu Bakr appointed Zaid Bin Thabith to collect the Qur'an. He describes it in this way:

> Narrated Zaid bin Thabit: Abu Bakr as-Siddiq sent for me when the people of Yamama had been killed . . . Then Abu Bakr said (to me): 'You are a wise young man and we do not have any suspicion about you, and you used to write the Divine Inspiration for Allah's Apostle. So you should search for (the fragmentary script of) the Qur'an and collect it (in one book). By Allah! If they had ordered me to shift one of the mountains, it would not have been heavier for me than this ordering me to collect the Qur'an. Then I said to Abu Bakr, 'How will you do something which Allah's Apostle did not do?' Abu Bakr replied, 'By Allah, It is a good project.'[15]

---

[14] Darwaza, *Al-Qur'an al-Majid*, p.54.
[15] *Sahih al-Bukhari*, Vol. 6, p.477.

Zaid eventually agreed to supervise the compilation. He is said to have collected the Qur'an from men's memories, date palms, white stones, etc. The completed text was kept by Abu Bakr and, after his death, by his successor Umar ibn al-Khattab (634–644). Upon Umar's death it passed to his daughter Hafsah (d.665).[16] This shows that it was not treated as an official copy; if it had been then, according to a set practice, they would have kept it in the office known as the treasury, *Baithulmal*. This tradition suggests that Abu Bakr collected the whole Qur'an into one book for the first time. It also implies that he made no critical study of the text with a view to reducing the various readings, and other private compilations to form one uniform standard. This collection did not receive any official publicity, simply because some prominent teachers of the Qur'an such as Ubay ibn Ka'b (d.639 or later), Abu Abdullah ibn Masood (d.653), Abu Musa Al-Ashari (d.662) and Miqdad ibn Amr (d.653) and other companions of Muhammad were still alive. Muhammad in his lifetime had acknowledged Ka'b and Masood as the foremost authorities on the Qur'an.[17] Perhaps this was the reason that Zaid's collection faded into virtual obscurity and went into the private custody of Hafsah.[18]

According to some traditions, Muhammad's son-in-law, Ali Ibn Abi Talib (d.661), had compiled his own copy of the Qur'an. He took it to Abu Bakr and Umar. However, they each refused to accept this version and told Ali that they were not in need of the version of the Qur'an collected by him. In anger Ali said, 'By God! you will never be able to see it after this day.'[19]

---

[16] Some, however, give the year of her death as 661–2; according to Ibn al-Athir it is 647–8 at the time when Marwan was governor of Madinah. (*Encyclopaedia of Islam*, Vol. III, p.65).

[17] *Sahih al-Bukhari*, Vol 5, p.96.

[18] *Sahih al-Bukhari*, Vol 6, p.478.

[19] *Usul-al-Kafi*, p.671 cited by Manzoor Nomani, *Irani Inqilab*, p.260.

Although the majority of Muslims accept that it was in Abu Bakr's time that the first collection was made, this assertion is contradicted by another account, according to which it was during the reign of Umar (634–644 CE) that the Qur'an was first collected. According to yet another tradition, it was not Abu Bakr but Umar who ordered the compilation, although he died before it was completed.[20]

It has also been argued that those who died in the battle of Yamama were mostly new converts and would not have known the Qur'an by heart. It is also strange that the copy prepared under Abu Bakr's control was not treated as an official copy, but almost as a private collection under Hafsah's safekeeping. This situation aroused some suspicion, so that some assert that the story of the first compilation under Abu Bakr was invented by those who disliked Uthman (see below). Yet others suggest that this story was invented 'to take the collection of the Qur'an back as near as possible to Muhammad's death' i.e. to gain respectability for the authenticity of the version of the Qur'an we have today.[21]

The Uthmanic recension

According to tradition, the next step towards an official Qur'an was taken under the 3rd caliph, Uthman (d.656). The discrepancies and contradictions which existed between the various readings of the Qur'an and copies of the companions of Muhammad became a grave cause of dissension among Muslims, not only in Makkah and

---

[20] Ibn Sa'd, *Tabaqat*, Vol 1/111, p.2124 cited by Abdur Rahman Doi, *Qur'an: An Introduction*, p.26.

[21] Adams, C.J., Quran: The Text and its History, '*Encylopedia of Religion*, Mircea Eliade (Ed.) [New York: Macmillan, 1987], pp.157–76.

Madinah but as far away as Iraq and Syria. This prompted Uthman, to take steps to suppress the doubts which had begun to arise in people's minds. Muslims disagreed about the variant editions of the Qur'an so much that we are told that 'during Uthman's time, pupils and teachers ended up killing each other. When Uthman found out about this, he said, "Here in my presence, you lie in the Qur'an and make it full of mistakes, so those who are in far away lands, they must be doing more than this".'[22]

Thus the Qur'an was first *officially* collated between 650 and 656 CE during Uthman's reign. There are several narratives describing how the official Qur'an was put together, but the one quoted most often by Muslim writers is that Uthman appointed a committee, comprising Zaid Bin Thabith and three other prominent Makkans to collate the Qur'an. He asked for the manuscript of the Qur'an that had been deposited with Hafsah. Zaid and his committee made use of this earlier copy and further corrected it wherever they decided it was necessary. Uthman then sent copies of this new, official compilation to every Muslim province and 'ordered that all other Qur'anic materials, whether written in fragmentary manuscripts or whole copies, be burnt.'[23]

This drastic action by Uthman is itself evidence that major textual differences existed between various copies of the Qur'an. Such differences were not only affecting the *qira* (recitation of the Qur'an) but also its form and content. Though Uthman was extremely successful in his destruction of the old manuscripts, evidence exists that variant traditions of the consonantal text survived among the learned. Indeed, a great mass of material can be collected regarding the variant readings in the texts of Ubayy,

---

[22] Suyuti, *Al-Itqan fi Ulum al-Qur'an*, Vol. 1, p.160.
[23] *Sahih al-Bukhari*, Vol. 6, p.479.

Ibn Masood and several others. These variants are quoted verbatim in the classical commentaries and other works written by eminent Muslim scholars of their day. Nowadays, many Muslims prefer to claim that the differences between these Qur'ans were only to be found in the pronunciation, in the recitation of the text:

> The variations which have become the subject-matter of discussion were not variations either of the text or verse or even variation of a word. They were all cases of enunciation of vowel points which did not in any way alter the meaning or significance of a word.[24]

If the difference only appeared in the verbal recital based on the same written text, why destroy it? The facts show that Uthman ordered the destruction of the *written* texts. Furthermore, there were neither vowel points nor even diacritical marks in the early written texts of the Qur'an. Therefore the difference in recital would never have appeared in the written manuscripts. It is therefore clear that Uthman was standardising one written text of the Qur'an at the expense of all other versions of the Qur'an, with variant texts 'to be officially promulgated as the *textus receptus* of the Muslims.'[25]

Early codices of the Qur'an

Although the major early Qur'anic manuscripts were destroyed, much of the information about them and their variants is available in Muslim traditions, classical commentaries and other books written by respected and

---

[24] Bashiruddin, *Introduction to the Study of the Holy Qur'an*, p.359.
[25] John Burton, *The Collection of the Qur'an*, p.138.

eminent Muslim divines. A study of these sources reveal that there were some fifteen codices that were affected by the decree of Uthman, including those belonging to companions of Muhammad, Ibn Masood and Ubay ibn Ka'b, Ali Ibn Abi Talib and Abu Musa. The Shia sect of Islam believes that Ali Ibn Abi Talib had compiled the real Qur'an and that it was different from the Uthmanic one. It remained in his possession and later passed on to his successors, the Imams. Many among them known as the *Ithna Ashari* (followers of the twelve Imams) believe that Ali's copy of the Qur'an is now with the 12th Imam, Abul Qasim Muhammad ibn Hasan, called al-Mahdi[26] who disappeared in 870. He is identified as the 'Hidden Imam' who will reveal Ali's copy on his reappearance.[27]

It seems that there were many among the companions of Muhammad who were not happy about the work of Zaid Bin Thabit and his colleagues. Among these were such people as Ibn Masood and Ali Ibn Abi Talib. Ibn Masood was one of the leading authorities on the Qur'anic text and one of the first Muslims to teach the Qur'an. He claimed to have recited more than seventy surahs of the Qur'an in Muhammad's presence.[28] Because of his ability and knowledge of the Qur'an, Muhammad

---

[26] A political adventurer named Mukhtar ibn Abi Ubaid (d.687) was the first to introduce the concept of the Mahdi (meaning the rightly-guided one). Some believe that the idea is similar to the biblical Messiah who would establish an ideal reign of absolute justice on earth. In later years the idea of the Mahdi took a firm hold in the Shia theology. Mahdi became an essential figure and was later identified as the Hidden Imam who will reappear and establish Islamic rule filling the world with righteousness. For a detailed Shia perspective: Jassim M. Hussain, *The Occultation of the Twelfth Imam: A Historical Background* (London: Muhammadi Trust, 1982).

[27] Manzoor Nomani, *Irani Inqilab*, p.258.

[28] *Sahih al-Muslim*, Vol. 4, p.1312.

specially recommended him as one of the four to whom his followers should go to learn the Qur'an:

> Narrated Masruq: Abdullah bin Masood was mentioned before Abdullah bin Amr who said, 'That is a man I still love, as I heard the Prophet saying, "Learn the Qur'an from four: from Abdullah Ibn Masood – he started with him – Salim, the freed slave of Abu Hudhaifa, Mu'dah bin Jabal, and Ubai bin Ka'b".'[29]

Ibn Masood's codex became the standard text for the Muslims in and around Kufa in Iraq before Uthman's standardisation. Despite the arrival of the official Uthmanic Qur'an, Abdullah Ibn Masood refused to abandon his own copy in its favour. The majority of Muslims at Kufa stood by him and his text. He advised them to hide their copies of the Qur'an, and not to give them up to destruction, in these words, '*Ya ahl al-Araaq, Aktumu al-Masahif al-lati indakum wa ghulquha*, O people of Iraq, hide your Qur'ans and shut them up under lock and key.'[30]

This action of Ibn Masood resulted in the withdrawal of his stipend. It is recorded that the caliph forcibly seized and burnt Ibn Masood's own Qur'an. One day this controversy so enraged Uthman that he ordered a servant to forcibly throw Ibn Masood out of the mosque, thereby breaking his ribs.[31] This was the behaviour shown towards a person about whom Muhammad had said, 'I am indeed pleased with one among my people with whom Ibn Masood is happy, and I am displeased with the one with whom Ibn Masood is displeased.'[32]

---

[29] *Sahih al-Bukhari*, Vol. 5, p.96.

[30] Ibn al-Athir, *Kamil*, Vol. III, 86–87, as cited by Khurshid, *Hazrat Usman ke Surkari Khatoot*.

[31] Khurshid Ahmad Khurshid, *Hazrat Usman ke Surkari Khatoot*, p.106.

[32] Shaikh Abdul Haqq, *Madarij-e-Nabbuwat*, p.852.

The Ummayad and Abbasid period

Muslim writers boldly allege: 'It is a truly miraculous fact that the text of the Qur'an has been preserved absolutely pure and entire, down to the last vowel point.'[33] Such a claim is not substantiated by the history of the Qur'anic text which shows that diacritical marks and vowel points were only fully introduced at least two hundred years after Muhammad's death.

In the light of Muslim traditions, an honest Muslim cannot deny the discrepancies in the Qur'an which even include disagreements over the number of copies that Uthman sent to Makkah, Syria, Yemen, Bahrain, Basra and Kufa. Some claimed there were five, others four, still others seven.[34] The copy sent to Makkah was burned in around 820. The copy sent to Madina was lost in the days of Yazid b.Muawiya (d.683). The copy sent to Iraq was lost in the days of Al-Mukhtar Ibn Abi Ubaid (d.687).

During the Abbasid period (750–1258?), the writing of books became a hallmark of Islamic culture, and the science and study of the Qur'an (*Ulum al-Qur'an*), was no exception. Several scholars wrote about the variant readings e.g. as found in either codices of companions of the prophet, or of the second generation of Muslims. However, many of these writings did not survive, due in the main to the rivalry and political requirements of those in power. In spite of this, a collation of variants considered during the Uthman recension still survives in the book *Kitab al-Masahif*, by Ibn Abi Dawood (d.928).[35]

---

[33] Zafrullah Khan, *Islam: Its Meaning for Modern Man*, p.89.

[34] Suyuti, *Al-Itqan fi Ulum al-Qur'an*, Vol. 1, p.162.

[35] Arthur Jeffery, *Materials for the history of the text of the Qur'an*. This book contains the *Kitab al-Masahif* of Ibn Abi Dawood together with a collection of the variant readings from the

It seems that Zaid's very first compilation, which initially remained in the possession of Hafsah, was considerably different from the Uthmanic canon prepared by Zaid and his committee. Such a difference is evident from the behaviour of Marwan Ibn al-Hakam (d.685), when he was governor of Madina. Despite many efforts, Hafsah refused to give him her manuscript of the Qur'an. In fact, after she died, Marwan sent his men to prise the book away from Hafsah's half brother, Abdallah Ibn Umar (d.693), who yielded eventually and sent it to Marwan, who then burnt it. No wonder Ibn Umar is reported to have said, 'Let no man say, I have learned the whole of the Qur'an! How can he have learned the whole of it when much of it has been lost? Let him say, I have learned what is present of it.'[36]

Text improvement and text uniformity

By the time of the Ummayyad caliph, Abd al-Malik (685–705), the inadequacy of the existing script led Muslims to improve on the text to make it easier to read for a wider community. Al-Hajjaj Ibn Yusaf (694–714), the viceroy of Iraq, is said to have directed the work. He was also accused of making changes in the text,[37] but his accusers were powerless to control the text. Ibn Abi Dawood lists these amendments in considerable detail in the chapter, *Ma Ghaira al-Hajjaj fi Mushaf Usman* – 'What was altered by Al-Hajjaj in the Uthmanic text.'[38] It is interesting to note

---

[35] (*continued*) codices of Ibn Masood, Ubai, Ali, Ibn Abbas, Anas, Abu Musa and other early Qur'anic authorities. It presents examples of text predating that of the canonical text of Uthman.

[36] Suyuti, *Al-Itqan fi Ulum al-Qur'an*, Vol 2. p.64.

[37] Qamar Naqvi, *Sahayef*, p.109.

[38] *Kitab al-Masahif*, p.117.

that coins uncovered from the time of Abdul Malik have Qur'anic writings on them which suggest variant readings. Furthermore, the quotation on the Dome of the Rock sanctuary (built by Abdul Malik in Jerusalem in 691) points to another variant reading. A comparison of these inscriptions with the text of the present Qur'an, suggest that, through the years, the Qur'an went through an evolution during its transmission.

The coming to power of the Abbasid dynasty in 750, when the new caliphs settled in Baghdad, coincided with the very thorough grammatical and analytical studies of the Torah and other parts of the Bible by both Jews and Christians. These trends in their studies also influenced some Muslims to attempt the same in the case of the Qur'an. It is no surprise that the first grammarian specialising in Arabic poetic metre is Khalil ibn Ahmad (d.791) of the school of Basra.

It seems clear in the light of the available collections of traditions and other indirect sources that the process of improving the text of the Qur'an was only completed towards the end of the ninth century. In the early tenth century, to enforce further uniformity, further very strict measures were taken. Until that time, scholars and theologians were free to use the Uthmanic recension as their main source but also to browse among the various versions for study and reference. This facility was known as *Ikhtiyar* (choice). However this *Ikhtiyar* did not confine itself to a choice from among the possible pointings of a standard consonantal text, but extended to choosing between different texts. In different districts, some of the variant readings of older codices were actually taught alongside the Uthmanic revised version. Some of these variations in the text started to appear in the writings of the teachers. This obviously caused dissension between various teachers and their associates. For example, the first person recorded to be concerned with the problem, and to have tried to bring uniformity, is said to be Malik Ibn Ans (d.795). He rejected several of the companions' versions, especially the version of Ibn Masood. Ibn Ans explicitly stated that it was invalid to perform *salah* (the five daily prayers) under the *imamah* (presiding) of someone who used the version of Ibn Masood.[39] However, it was only in the year 934, that Ibn Mujahid (859–935) at Baghdad was authorised to define the only official permissible readings of the Qur'an. He achieved this through his influence with two of the *wazirs* (ministers), Ibn Isa and Ibn Muqlah, in the Abbasid government.

The first step Ibn Mujahid took was to write a book entitled, *Al-qira'at as-saba*, 'The seven readings'. He based his scholarship on a tradition that Muhammad had allowed the recitation of the Qur'an according to seven *ahruf* (letters). Although the tradition does detail what those seven methods are, Ibn Mujahid interpreted it as reciting the Qur'an in seven different *ways*. For this purpose, he chose (at his own discretion) seven of the many sets of readings that were in use in various districts and declared them to be the authorised readings. The sets of 'readings' were in fact different versions, one each from Ibn Kathir (d.737) from Makkah, Nafi (d.785) of Madina, Ibn Amir (d.736) of Damascus and Abu Amr (d.770) of Basra and three were of Asim (d.744), Hamzah (d.772) and al-Kisai (d.804) from Kufa. Ibn Mujahid introduced not only a definite process of forming a canon but also prohibited the use of any other Iikhtiyar (choice) or other variations in the text except the seven readings he had selected.[40] Furthermore, there were two different versions for each set of readings, making fourteen versions in all.

---

[39] Watt & R. Bell, *Introduction to the Qur'an*, p.48.
[40] Arthur Jeffery, Progress in the Study of the Qur'an Text, p.9 in *The Muslim World*, (1935), No. 1.

Pressure to conform

Very soon, several scholars were publicly forced to renounce their preference for other collections and variations. Among these were people like Ibn Miqsam[41] and Ibn Shanabudh (d.939) who were condemned to prison and forced to give up their own versions of the Qur'an including the versions of Ibn Masood and Ibn Kab. The codex of Ali ibn Abi Talib was also rejected.[42] In his *Kitab al-Fihrist*, Abu al-Faraj Muhammad Ibn Ishaq al-Nadim (d.990) records some of the variants in Ibn Shanabudh's version of the Qur'an. Al-Nadim mentions Shanabudh's admission of being wrong and consequent repentance. He was not released, however, and later died in prison.[43]

Ibn Mujahid's system marked a change in the way that early readings of the Qur'an were studied. Although his system was accepted, during subsequent years, all but two of the fourteen versions were dropped. The only two versions to survive with modification to this present century are claimed to be those of Hafs (d.796) and Warsh (d.812). Even among these two, it is the Hafs (the revised reading of Asim) that is now widely used in practice: it has acquired canonical supremacy except in west and northwest Africa where the transmission of Warsh (the revised reading of Nafi) is often used.[44]

Many Muslims are completely unaware that the Qur'an has this history. Of those who do know about it, several nevertheless deny the existence of variants in the Qur'an; others claim, as we have said, that all variations

---

[41] Or Ibn Muqsim; he was also known as Abu Bakr al-Attar.

[42] Watt & R. Bell, *Introduction to the Qur'an*, p.49.

[43] *The Fihrist of al-Nadim*, Vol. 1, pp.70–72.

[44] Adrian Brockett, 'The value of the Hafs and Warsh transmissions for the textual history of the Qur'an', in *Approaches to the History of the Interpretation of the Qur'an*, p.31.

were only cases of enunciation of vowel points which did not in any way alter the meaning or significance of a word.[45] Available research, however, shows that the difference in the copies of the Qur'an was more than just that of spelling, choice of synonyms or use of particles, etc.[46]

Conclusion

Going through the available information, we find that the oldest surviving text of the Qur'an originates not earlier than about one and a half centuries after Muhammad's death.

The traditional idea that the Qur'an is preserved 'word for word' and 'letter for letter' is baseless. There were disagreements among the companions of Muhammad and Muslims of the classical era about the text of the Qur'an, its compilation and variant readings. The Qur'an suffered from variant readings, additions and omissions which were later officially suppressed.

The Qur'an we have today does not represent the whole of its message although we may still believe that its essential substance is preserved.

The present Qur'an is not entirely the same as that from the time of Muhammad nor is it a fully fledged copy of the Uthmanic recension. The Qur'an was revised by Ibn Mujahid (about 250 years after Uthman), and has undergone a process of further refinement, resulting in the canon we have today.

---

[45] Bashiruddin, *Introduction to the Study of the Holy Qur'an*, p.359.
[46] Ahmad von Denffer, *Ulum Al-Qur'an*, p.47.

3

Evidence of reliability (2)

In the previous chapter we looked for evidence relating to the reliability of the Qur'an, a document which most Muslims claim was received during 23 years (610–632) by one prophet. We will now consider the Bible, which is also known to us as the Old and the New Testaments. The Bible was put together over a period of about 1,500 years (1,450 BCE – 100 CE).

The text of the Old Testament

Any keen reader of the Old Testament is soon made aware that the Hebrew text translated refers to the so-called 'Masoretic' text.[1] This was the basic text of the Old Testament, used for centuries in schools and synagogues. It was collected by the Masoretes, schools of rabbis in Palestine and in Babylonia. These schools played a major part in the collection of the many copies of the text. In these schools, scribes produced manuscripts of the agreed 'best text' in the form which scholars now know it. (One may say that their process of recension was similar to that carried out

[1] A small part of the Old Testament is in Aramaic. Some portions, which are used by the Catholic and Orthodox Church are known as 'apocrypha', have texts preserved in Greek.

on the Qur'anic texts by the commission of Uthman and later by Hajjaj and Ibn Mujahid.)

To the original consonantal text the scholars added vowel pointing to help readers in the synagogues. In the margins, they also added notes (*Masora* or *Tafsir*) on the text. It was their activity that gave us the many copies of this text which have survived and are now available round the world. Some of these manuscripts are held in college libraries in Oxford and Cambridge universities. The most famous family of the Masoretes were the Ben Asher family, who worked in Tiberias from the late eighth to the mid-tenth centuries.

Until 1947, the oldest Hebrew document that was available to us was the Nash Papyrus, a fragment measuring 3 by 5 inches, dated to between 100 BCE to 70 CE, inscribed with the Ten Commandments and the *Shema*, a prayer from the book of Deuteronomy. Another collection of fragments is called 'The Geniza Fragments'. These are 200,000 fragments of biblical texts in Hebrew and Aramaic. This collection also contains other Jewish religious and non-religious literature texts. The earliest date for the Old Testament text in this collection is from the fifth century CE. Apart from that, the oldest surviving Hebrew scripts were Masoretic codices of the Prophets. They are: Cairo (895 CE); Leningrad (916 CE) and a full Old Testament codex known as the Aleppo Codex from the tenth century. Both the Leningrad and the Aleppo codices can be traced indirectly to the last two members of the Masoretes, the Bani Ashir: Moses bin Ashir and his son Aaron bin Moses ben Ashir.

Muslims in their discussions and writings have never accepted the value of the Masoretic texts saying that they were put together very late, long after Muhammad, the prophet of Islam. However, since the discovery of the Dead Sea Scrolls, earlier evidence of biblical records has

Figure 7. The Isaiah Scroll

IQIsᵃ Isaiah 53 as found in the Dead Sea Scrolls.
(Picture produced by permission of Israel Museum)

come to light. This discovery at Qumran (1947–56) has
unveiled to us some five hundred whole or incomplete
books, which were copied during the period about 275
years before Christ to about 65 years after him.[2] Among
these are one hundred Hebrew Old Testament texts dating
from the first century BCE to the first century CE. All the
books of the Old Testament except Esther are among
them. In these scrolls researchers now have access to
manuscripts in Hebrew that are a thousand years older
than previously available. Many of the texts are very close
to the Masoretic text. The Isaiah scroll for example

---

[2] Metzger and Coogan, *The Oxford Companion to the Bible*,
pp.500–501 (Oxford: 1993).

contains the complete Bible book of Isaiah. It is an enormous work, made out of seventeen sheets of leather sewn together side by side to make a scroll measuring almost 8 metres in length, and about 26 centimetres high. The whole find provides strong evidence that the Hebrew text of the Bible, in all essentials, is identical to the original prose. It also proves that the Old Testament text was not changed before or after the time of Muhammad, as many Muslims have asserted.

The lists of Old Testament books

How can one know which books are worthy to be part of the Bible, and which are not? For that purpose Christians refer to lists of the books of the Old Testament. These lists predate Muhammad. The three main ones are by Josephus (d.90), the Council of Jamnia (75–117) and the Council of Laodicea (363). Josephus was a Jewish historian who wrote for a Greek and Roman audience to defend the Jewish people as a people of faith.[3] The council of Jamnia was an assembly of Jewish elders who listed the Old Testament books that they recognised as 'Scripture'. Similarly the Council of Laodicea was held by the Christian Church, and listed not only the books of the Old Testament but also those of the New Testament considered worthy for use in teaching and worship.

These lists all show that the Jews, as 'people of the book', knew the contents of the Scriptures they had received. There are many other lists found in the writings of early Christians, even of those treated as heretics. There are a few variations between lists, in part because of their heretical purpose or some other reservations. Some lists have represented some of the longer books as having been

---

[3] *The Work of Josephus, Against Apion*, Book 1, chapter 8, p.787.

subdivided, thus inflating the total number of Old Testament books to 55 or 57. In spite of these exceptions, all Christian Churches accept the 39 books of the Protestant Old Testament Canon, which is the essential core of the Old Testament. Others have also included a few other small documents as well but still treating them as Apocrypha (see Appendix 1). In spite of these exceptions the majority of them agree with the 39 books as present in our present-day Old Testament.

Translations of the Old Testament

Many translations of the Old Testament, prepared by both Christians and Jews, predate Muhammad. Here are the main examples: the Greek version known as the Septuagint was prepared in Egypt (285–200 BCE) of which a manuscript, the Codex Vaticanus from the fourth or fifth century is in the Vatican library; (see illustration 8) Aquila's Version in 130 by a Jew living in what is now Turkey; the Symmachus' Version in the year 170, translated by a Jew in Palestine; and Theodotion's Version (150–200).

Among the Latin versions done by Christians are the Old Latin Version (100–200) which was a translation of the Septuagint. A later translation called the Vulgate was made by Jerome from the original Hebrew and Aramaic. Jerome's work was approved in the year 405.

Among the Syriac translations were the Peshitta (100–300) and the Philoxenian (500). Among the Coptic versions, the best known are the Sahidic (250); the Akhmimic (250–350) and the Bohairic (300). There is also a Gothic version (4th century).

There were several other translations that were made long before Muhammad: they are the Ethiopic (300); the Armenian (411); the Georgian (500) and the Nubian (500s).

Figure 8. Codex Vaticanus

The three-column codex Vaticanus, from the fourth or fifth century CE. It is one of the oldest copies of the Greek translation known as the Septuagint.

Although the dates of the work are known, we do not have pre-Muhammad copies of these versions.

One can go into further detail but the above list is sufficient to prove the point that long before Muhammad's time the Old Testament in Hebrew had many translations, which were widely available in Africa, the Middle East, Central Asia, Asia Minor and Western Europe.

The evidence for the New Testament

Following Jesus' command to make disciples, Christianity has always been a missionary faith (Matthew 28:19–20;

Acts 1:5–7). It seems clear from the information available that Jesus' disciples believed it was the Holy Spirit who enabled them to proclaim and put into writing what Jesus had said and done. Jesus himself had promised to send the Holy Spirit to remind them of the things he had taught. His words were, 'He shall guide you unto all the truth' (John 14:26; 16:13). Thus, by the end of the second century, copies of the books of the New Testament were valued possessions within the communities of believers. So Christians today not only have the teaching of Jesus, but also the narrative of his mighty works, that is, the twofold witness of the disciples. The disciples of Jesus did not add any new doctrine to his teaching. They merely wrote out of the conviction given by the Holy Spirit.

The Christian Church soon accepted these writings as inspired. By the second century, there were those who opposed the apostles, and there were even some who compiled their own 'Gospels', adding various unorthodox teachings. Conversely, others left out certain parts, exactly as happened in the case of the early collections of the Qur'an. However, just as the majority of Muslims stick to the Qur'an that they have today, the majority of Christians stick to the canon of the Bible that they have today.

Christians claim that by the end of 120 CE, the writing and compilation of the New Testament was finished. There is historical evidence that, by this time, the four gospels of Matthew, Mark, Luke and John, were circulating widely, which would normally indicate that they were compiled long before this time. A Syrian Christian called Tatian, who lived around the middle of the second century, took the trouble to turn these four Gospels into a single continuous narrative. This work was known as the *Diatessaron*[4] and enjoyed considerable popularity for a

---

[4] F.F. Bruce, *The New Testament Documents: Are they reliable?*, p.23.

time. One of the Syriac fathers, Ephrem (306–373), wrote a commentary on the *Diatessaron*, which is still extant in its entirety in an Armenian translation. Two thirds of his Syriac original are found in the Chester Beatty collection.[5] These facts suggest that at this time the four Gospels were recognised as uniquely authoritative.

The earliest documents

Many ancient books such as Homer's *Iliad*; Suetonius' *De Vita Caesarum*, Caesar's *Gallic Wars* only exist in copies made long after the date of writing. For example the time gap between Homer (900 BCE) and the oldest copy of his *Iliad* is some five hundred years and that between Suetonius (75–160) and his work *De Vita Caesarum* is about eight hundred years. Nonetheless scholars do not doubt the historicity of the texts. (In the case of the Qur'an, the earliest manuscript available to us is one dated 140 years later than Muhammad's death.[6])

Until the seventeenth century, the only widely available text of the Greek New Testament was one of Byzantine origin dating from some time after the sixth century. Other manuscripts then came to light. Now there are about 5,300 Greek manuscripts still in existence which contain all or part of the New Testament. There are 10,000 Latin texts, and 9,300 other early versions available. This totals more than 24,000 manuscript copies of portions of the New Testament. A considerable number of them were written long before the compilation of the Qur'an and the rise of Islam.

Among all the Greek manuscripts, about fifty are complete copies of the New Testament. Of the remainder around two thousand contain just the text of the gospels.

---

[5] F.F. Bruce, *The Canon of the Scriptures*, p.128.
[6] Ahmad von Denffer, *Ulum Al-Qur'an*, pp.60–61.

The epistles are found together with Acts in about 400 copies; while Paul's epistles alone appear in about 300 copies. There are 250 or so copies of the book of Revelation available.

Two important early manuscripts are the Codex Alexandrinus,[7] written in the fifth century, and the Codex Bezae, written in the fifth or possibly sixth century. The former is in the British Museum in London and the latter in the University library at Cambridge. The Codex Bezae has Latin and Greek texts of the Gospels and Acts on facing pages. It includes a small fragment of 3 John.[8] The Codex Sinaiticus, which dates from the fourth century, contains the entire New Testament and part of the Old Testament in Greek.[9] Another manuscript, the Codex Vaticanus[10] was produced in the fourth century. Some scholars suggest that this manuscript is slightly older than the Codex Sinaiticus. However, others believe that both manuscripts were originally among the fifty copies of the Scriptures prepared due to a request by the emperor in about 331 CE.[11]

The Codex Ephraimi was written in the 5th century, but the vellum was scraped and reused in the 12th century (a normal procedure in those days). Through the use of special chemicals and ultraviolet light, scholars have deciphered the earlier writing of the 5th century. The Codex Ephraimi contains sixty-four leaves from the Old Testament and one hundred and forty-five of the New Testament representing about 60 per cent of the New Testament text.

---

[7] F.F. Bruce, *The Canon of the Scriptures*, p.69, 206.

[8] Metzger, *The Text of the New Testament*, p.49.

[9] F.F. Bruce, *The New Testament Documents: Are they reliable?*, p.16.

[10] F.F. Bruce, *The Canon of the Scriptures*, p.69, 206.

[11] Metzger, *The Text of the New Testament*, p.44.

Figure 9. Codex Sinaiticus

A page from the Codex Sinaiticus dated from 350CE. The passage is John 21:1–25.

(Produced by permission from the British Library)

So far a few of the manuscripts that date from the 4th and 5th centuries are mentioned. A considerable number of papyrus fragments also exist written 100–200 years earlier. The earliest surviving collection of the Gospels is Papyrus P45, which contains part of the text of the Gospels and Acts. One part is in the Chester Beatty collection in Dublin while the other is in the Austrian National Library in Vienna. P45 has been dated and accepted as early 3rd century, that is, soon after 200 CE. There are several other ancient papyri of the New Testament. For example, P46, the second Chester Beatty Papyrus, dates from the 3rd century. The third, P47, is part of the book of Revelation. Papyrus P66 is part of the Bodmer collection and consists of a substantial part of the Gospel of John (the first

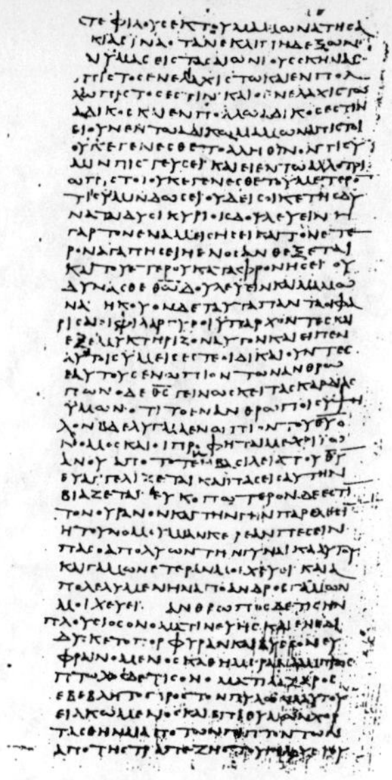

Figure 10. Bodmer Papyrus

A page from Bodmer Papyrus XIV [P75]. The passage is Luke 16:9–21

fourteen chapters are almost complete, while the rest are fragmentary). This codex was written about 200 CE. P72, P74 and P75 are also part of the Bodmer collection. P75 contains parts of Luke and John, also dated 200.

The Papyrus fragment of the Gospel according to John, P52, in the John Ryland's library, in the University of Manchester, is dated 120, some twenty-five years after John's Gospel was written.

An interesting example among the Dead Sea Scrolls found at Qumran is a fragment known as 7Q5. A German scholar and Papyrologist, Carsten Thiede, following a Spanish Jesuit scholar Jose O' Callaghan's findings, believes that this fragment is of the Gospel according to Mark and is pre 68 CE. He also claims that the *Magdalene Manuscript*, in Oxford, a fragment from

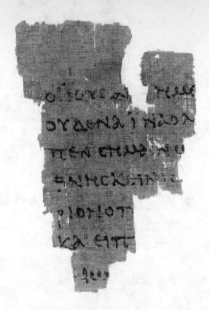

Figure 11. Greek Papyrus 457
A fragment of John's Gospel, dates from 125–150 CE.

the Gospel according to Matthew, was written around 66 CE. This would mean that this manuscript was written, at the latest, within thirty-five years of Jesus' death, possibly earlier, and dates from a time when eyewitnesses to Gospel events were still alive.[12] Thiede's findings have not yet been widely accepted, and the research and debate go on.[13]

---

[12] Carsten Peter Thiede, *Rekindling the Word: In Search of Gospel Truth*, Pennsylvania: 1995. See also: Thiede, *Time*, April 29, 1996, p.8.

[13] For a rebuttal see: Graham Stanton, *Gospel Truth? New Light on Jesus & the Gospels*, Pennsylvania: 1995. Carsten responds to some of Stanton's objections in his other book, *The Jesus Papyrus*, London: Weidenfeld & Nicolson, 1996.

Early translations of the New Testament

In the very early days, translations were also made into other languages to enable people from other regions to understand the new Christian faith. As time passed, Greek also ceased to be the common language for the majority of Christians. As it was never considered an essential part of faith that a Christian should learn Greek and Hebrew to study the Scriptures, we see that translations were regarded as useful from the beginning. Along with translation of the Old Testament, Christians continued to translate the New Testament into other languages. There are, therefore, about 15,000 copies of various early translations or versions of the New Testament still extant. A few are bound with the Old Testament translations.

Some of these translations are in Latin, written as early as 150 CE. By the third century many old Latin versions circulated in North Africa and Europe. Others were written in Syriac such as the Peshitta, and produced around 150–250.[14] As there are Syriac versions of the Old Testament, a translation for the New Testament was also prepared. The old Syriac version of the four Gospels is preserved in two manuscripts copied in about the fourth and fifth centuries. The form of the text is said to be from the second or the beginning of the third century.

The Peshitta version of the New Testament section of the Bible was prepared about the beginning of the fifth century. More than 350 manuscripts of Peshitta New Testament are known today, several of which date from the fifth and sixth centuries.

---

[14] McDowell, *Evidence that Demands a Verdict*, p.49.

Other translations are: Coptic (300), Armenian (circa 400)[15], Gothic (4th century)[16], Georgian (5th century), Philoxenian (circa 500)[17], Ethiopic (6th century)[18] and Nubian (6th century)[19]. Not only were all these translations produced before the rise of Islam, we should also note that if somebody at any time wanted to corrupt them, they would have had to go to *all* of them to alter them – a completely impossible task.

The evidence of the lectionaries

Lectionaries (from the Latin *lectum*, to read) are books that contain selections of passages from the Bible intended for reading during worship (or reciting as Muslims might say)[20]. So far 2280 of these manuscripts have been catalogued, among which are 2135 lectionaries that contain passages from the New Testament, gospel portions together with parts of Acts and the epistles. Although many of these are from the tenth to thirteenth centuries, a few are earlier, leading some scholars to postulate that the lectionary system originated around the fourth century.[21] Like Islamic commentaries, these reinforce evidence for the text existing at these early dates in the same form as later texts.

---

[15] There is some reason to think that the earliest Armenian version of the Gospels circulated in the form of *Diatessaron*.

[16] The Gothic translation is the earliest known literary document in a Germanic dialect.

[17] F.F. Bruce, *The Canon of the Scriptures*, p.215.

[18] Some argue for a date as early as the fourth century (Metzger, *The Text of the New Testament*, p.84).

[19] McDowell, *Evidence that Demands a Verdict*, p.50.

[20] Metzger, *The Text of the New Testament*, p.30.

[21] Kurt and Barbara Aland, *The Text of the New Testament*, pp.166–167.

The evidence of the early Christian writings

There are many witnesses for the authority of the New Testament manuscripts from the early Christian writers. Some of these are known as the Apostolic Fathers from the 2nd and 3rd centuries CE. A great many copies of their writings have been preserved, many of which are literally filled with quotations of the Scriptures, the number of which exceeds 86,000.[22] This shows that they possessed copies of the Scriptures which were older than some of the manuscripts available to us today. They not only recognised the New Testament as Scripture but also testified to the unique authority of it.

As an example, a letter attributed to the Jewish Christian Barnabas recognises the integrity of the gospel according to Matthew by referring to it with the words, *'It is written'*.[23] Note that Jews used this particular expression only when quoting from books they regarded as inspired.[24] This formula was adopted by Christians when they referred to a passage or passages from the Scriptures both of the Jews and Christians.[25] In the Barnabas letter, there are quotations from other parts of the New Testament referring to the miracles of Christ, his crucifixion, death, resurrection and ascension.

Clement of Rome (d.100) was one of the co-workers of the apostles (Philippians 4:3). He wrote a letter to the Church at Corinth in about 95 CE[26] in which he quoted both from Jesus and the apostles using the text of the New Testament; the documents existed in his time and were available to the churches in the area. Similarly one may

---

[22] McDowell, *Evidence that Demands a Verdict*, p.52.

[23] Epistle of Barnabas 4:14 referring to Matthew 22:14.

[24] J.N.D. Kelly, *Early Christian Doctrine*, p.56.

[25] F.F. Bruce, *The Canon of the Scriptures*, p.65,126–127.

[26] F.F. Bruce, *The Books and the Parchments*, p.63.

cite from Ignatius (50–115), the bishop of Antioch, who died as a martyr. He treated the four gospel narratives as one and referred to them as 'the Gospel,' an authoritative writing.[27] In his letters, there are identifiable quotations from Matthew, John, Romans, First and Second Corinthians, Galatians, Ephesians, Philippians, First and Second Timothy, Titus and possible allusions to Mark, Luke, Acts, Colossians, Second Thessalonians, Philemon, Hebrews and First Peter.[28]

Polycarp (69–166) was a disciple of John the apostle. In one of his treatises, he quotes some 40 items from various parts of the New Testament. He mentions Christ's teaching, his crucifixion, death, resurrection and ascension. He talks about the hardship the apostles faced and how they still continued to preach and teach about Christ. Polycarp was martyred in 166.[29]

A well-known figure in the second century was Papias, bishop of Hierapolis around 110. He seems to have met Polycarp and John the apostle. In his writings he quotes from all four accounts of the gospel with references from the epistles of Peter, John, the Acts of the Apostles and Revelation.[30] Though Papias' writings have not survived, they are known from quotations in the work of others, notably Eusebius (d.340).

In the same era, in about 140, we meet another well-known figure, Justin Martyr. He was a knowledgeable man of his time who had studied not only religion but also the philosophies of Pythagoras and Plato. He wrote several books in defence of the Christian faith. He mentions all four accounts of the gospel of Jesus. In his *Dialogue with Trypho*, he repeatedly uses the phrase 'it is

---

[27] F.F. Bruce, *The New Testament Documents: Are they reliable?* p.23.

[28] F.F. Bruce, *The New Testament Documents: Are they reliable?* p.18.

[29] F.F. Bruce, *The New Testament Documents: Are they reliable?* p.18.

[30] F.F. Bruce, *The Canon of the Scriptures*, pp.2124–126.

written' when quoting from the New Testament Scriptures.

Another writer whose evidence is also very important is Irenaeus. In 180 he became the bishop of Lyon. In all his writings, the Scriptures play a dominant part. There is no mention of 'a list of New Testament books, but it is evident that he had a clear notion of their identity.'[31] His writings confirm the canonical recognition of all four narratives of the gospel. Referring to Irenaeus, Bruce states:

> In his treatise, Against Heresies, III, ii, 8, it is evident that by AD 180 the idea of the fourfold Gospel had become so axiomatic throughout Christendom that it could be referred to as an established fact as obvious and inevitable and natural as the four cardinal points of the compass (as we call them) or the four winds.[32]

In the third century Origen (185–254) mentions the four gospels, Acts and the epistles. In the fourth century, Athanasius (in 367) ratified the 27 books of the New Testament as canonical. Jerome (347–420) and Augustine (354–430) expressed similar views. Many more leading Christians of the first four centuries could be mentioned who quote extensively from the Scriptures. Their quotations from the New Testament are so many that the New Testament could almost be reconstructed from them alone without the use of the manuscripts.[33] That is exactly what an enthusiast, Sir David Dalrymple, did. Using only second and third century writings, he found the entire New Testament as quoted in the existing works of the Fathers, apart from a mere eleven verses.[34]

---

[31] F.F. Bruce, *The Canon of the Scriptures*, p.173.

[32] F.F. Bruce, *The Books and the Parchments*, p.109.

[33] Metzger, *The Text of the New Testament*, p.86.

[34] McDowell, *Evidence that Demands a Verdict*, p.51.

When such a wealth of evidence and textual attestation is compared with other works and their surviving manuscripts, one may conclude that no other work approaches the same standard as textual homogeneity of the Bible.

Circumstantial evidence

In the light of circumstantial evidence, a conservative estimate suggests that most of the New Testament was written before 70 CE. Several events in the late first century had a traumatic impact on the new Christian community, such as the fall of Jerusalem, the great fire of Rome and the subsequent persecution of Christians. Though there are probable allusions to the fall of Jerusalem in Matthew 13:14 and Luke 21:20–24, not one of these events is actually mentioned or recorded in any of the New Testament writings, despite their enormous impact on the Christian communities at the time. Furthermore, the martyrdom of James[35] in 62, of Paul in 64 and Peter in 65 are not mentioned at all, which indicates that these documents were written before these events had occurred. The very existence of the manuscripts, both full and incomplete, are also evidence of miraculous preservation, because within twenty years of the beginning of the Christian community, the Roman Emperor Nero (d.68) started a major state-sponsored persecution against Christians which continued on and off for the next two hundred and fifty years. In particular, in 303, Emperor Diocletian ordered that all Christian Scriptures should be burned. In spite of these campaigns of oppression the Scriptures survived.[36]

---

[35] James the brother of Jesus (Matthew 13:55). He became an important member of the Church (Galatians 1:19; Acts 12:17). The High priest, Hananiah, had him stoned to death. The death of another James, the apostle (44 CE) is recorded in Acts 12:2.
[36] F.F. Bruce, *The Spreading Flame*, p.185.

We notice that copies of the Old Testament and of the Qur'an are relatively few when compared with the New Testament material. The scarcity in the case of the Old Testament manuscript arises because the Jews looked upon their copies of the Scriptures with an almost superstitious respect, which led them to give ceremonial burial or cremation to any copy which was too old or became worn. Their motive was to prevent the improper use of the material on which the sacred name of God had been inscribed. This intention and custom deprived us of many early Hebrew manuscripts. The Dead Sea scrolls are a superb example of this custom of burial. In the case of the Muslims, there was a decree ordering the destruction of all the unofficial texts of the Qur'an as described in the previous chapter. Whether Muslims adopted the custom of burying or burning very old copies of the Qur'an is still open to debate.

One may ask why most of the New Testament manuscripts do not contain the *entire* New Testament? The simple reason could be that a hand written copy of the whole was both too bulky and too expensive for practical use. The available manuscripts show that working copies of the New Testament usually consisted of one of four parts of the whole collection:

1. The four Gospels
2. Acts and general epistles
3. Paul's letters
4. The Book of Revelation.

Very often groups 2, 3 and 4 were combined into one, to form a second volume, with the four gospels naturally serving as the first volume. In other words the New Testament was often broken down into separate volumes, explaining why most of the early manuscripts extant today do not contain all of the 27 books. Nevertheless there are more than 230 manuscripts containing the New Testament that still exist, and which date from the time before the Prophet of Islam and the start of Qur'anic Scripture.

The evidence from within the available compilation

So far, we have considered the external evidence for the reliability of transmission. Also available is the internal evidence from within passages of both the Old and the New Testament which shows how the preservation of its content began as far back as Moses. We find from consideration of these collections that God's message and the consequences of obeying or disobeying it, were presented in several forms:

1. Direct speech by God.
2. His words spoken by his chosen people in their own words.
3. God's words written (usually) through the prophets and their scribes.
4. Historical accounts and proverbial wisdom.

We also find that God's commands to most of his prophets were not merely to 'recite' – *Iqra*, but also to go and tell – *Qul*. They were often told to 'write down', *Uktubu* – a word which is *not* found in the Qur'an, requiring a written form to be created (see Jeremiah 30:2; Isaiah 30:8; Exodus 34:27). Thus there was transmission of the Bible text by both oral and written tradition. For example, in the period known as the Patriarchal Dispensation, God spoke directly to such people as Adam, Noah, Abraham and Joseph. But then the time came for this revelation to be preserved for humankind by means of a written record. The first person mentioned in the Bible as *writing* anything is Moses. In the early books of the Bible, there are seven distinct things directly attributed to Moses' hand. They are the memorial concerning Amalek (Exodus 17:14), the words of the covenant made at Sinai (Exodus 24:4), the ten commandments (Exodus 20), the journeys of the children of Israel in the wilderness (Numbers 33:2), the Book of the Law which was to be kept with the Ark of the covenant (Deuteronomy 31:9,24) and the hymn in Deuteronomy 32:1–43 (31:22) and Psalm 90. Moses is held to be the author of the first five books of the Bible. Other writers of the Bible and Jesus himself gave unvarying support to this view (Joshua 8:31; Judges 3:4; Malachi 4:4; Luke 24:44; John 7:19). The Torah mentions Moses commanding the appointed priests, 'Take this book of the law and place it beside the ark of the covenant of the Lord your God, that it may remain there as witness against you' (Deuteronomy 31:26).

Moses appointed Joshua according to God's command to succeed him as leader of Israel. About him it is written, 'Joshua recorded these things in the book of the law of God. Then he took a large stone and set it up there under the oak near the sanctuary of the Lord' (Joshua 24:26). Once divine revelation was put in writing, it was natural for other revelations and events to be recorded. Accordingly, Joshua as the successor of Moses also wrote words 'in the book of the law of God'. This in turn became the practice of other men of God who, through the inspiration of God, wrote both history and prophecy.

God chose Samuel as a prophet when David was a newborn infant. The instructions Samuel received from God were not only passed on verbally but, also, Samuel 'wrote them down on a scroll' (1 Samuel 10:25). Similarly Solomon's Proverbs are preserved (Proverbs 25:1).

Josiah, a king of Israel after David and Solomon, sought to reform his people. The record of his reforms commences: 'that he might confirm the words of the law

written in the book that Hilkiah the priest found in the
house of the Lord' (2 Kings 23:24). This proves that after
the time of David and Solomon, though many Israelites
had lapsed into idolatry, they still had the written law of
Moses in their possession.

The Prophet Jeremiah predicted the Babylonian conquest of the Jews and their transportation to Babylon and
their return to their own land after seventy years. Jeremiah dictated to his scribe Baruch Ibn Neriah, and the
Bible thus contains in writing what this prophet received
from God (Jeremiah 45:1).

Another example is Daniel who comments on what God
had revealed to Jeremiah. He says, 'I, Daniel, observed in
the books the number of the years which was revealed as
the word of the Lord to Jeremiah the prophet ...' (Daniel
9:2). Such a statement is clear evidence of the Scriptures
being preserved; these people retained access to the Scriptures in their possession despite being captives in exile.

Ezra was appointed as a scribe in around 400 BCE. The
Bible says that he was 'skilled in the law of Moses, which
the Lord God of Israel had given ...' (Ezra 7:6). He could not
have been a student of the Mosaic law if it had not been
available. He would not have been able to make further
copies of the law and the books of the prophets and chronicles if they were not there. The law of Moses was subse-
quently read in rebuilt Jerusalem (Nehemiah 8:1–8). So it is
seen that the Israelites preserved their Scriptures, to record
for posterity the way that God's hand was evident as he
sought to protect them throughout their history.

The testimonies of Jesus and the apostles

Jesus used passages from the Old Testament in his preaching and teaching. His first sermon in the synagogue was

based on a passage from the book of Isaiah (Luke 4:16,17). Although he accused the Jews of his time of wrongly interpreting the texts of the Scriptures, he never once accused them of corrupting that text. He accepted the authority of these Scriptures by referring to them. He not only observed them but also claimed that he came to fulfil what was prophesied about himself in them. Christians claim that in his birth, in his teaching, in his death and resurrection, Jesus fulfilled them in a precise manner, as predicted. To prove the point, after his resurrection, Jesus is reported to have explained what had happened from the Scriptures, 'the law of Moses, the prophets and the psalms' (Luke 24:44). Christians believe that this incident proves that Jesus believed the Scriptures of the Jews, known to us as the Old Testament, and thought of them as trustworthy.

Christians claim that God kept the Scriptures safe in the past and will continue to do so because he wants them preserved for the coming generations. Both the Bible and the Qur'an claim that God's words last forever. The prophet Isaiah says: 'The grass withers and the flowers fall, but the word of our God stands for ever.' (Isaiah 40:8). David states in the Psalms: 'The words of the Lord are flawless, like silver refined in a furnace of clay, purified seven times' (Psalm 12:6). Similarly, Peter, an apostle of Jesus quoting from Isaiah says, 'All men are like grass, and all their glory is like the flowers of the field; the grass withers and the flowers fall, but the word of the Lord stands forever' (1 Peter 1:24–25). Before his departure from the world, Peter said this to fellow believers, 'We did not follow cleverly invented stories when we told you about the power and coming of our Lord Jesus Christ, but we were eyewitnesses of his majesty' (2 Peter 1:16). About the Scriptures and the prophecies contained within it, he said, 'men spoke from God as they were carried along by the

Holy Spirit' (2 Peter 1:21). When preaching, both John, Peter and the other apostles, testified that the events and the teaching of Jesus were true; John said, 'We proclaim to you what we have seen and heard, so that you also may have fellowship with us' (1 John 1:3).

So where do we stand?

The available manuscripts and other documentary evidence show that the Bible text is reliable. Copies of the Old Testament as we have it were in existence before Jesus. As for the New Testament, we have evidence of manuscripts for the full text from about 125 years after Jesus and of the evidence of fragmentary manuscripts which show that the New Testament existed in written form about 40 years after Jesus. However, we must not ignore the fact that not everything Jesus (and many other prophets) said or taught through their actions is preserved in the Bible today. In the case of Jesus, one of his disciples testifies that Jesus did many other things which are not recorded. However, he gives his reason for the things that are included, that people may believe in Jesus and be partakers of the eternal life that is presented to them by God through Christ (John 20:30; 21:25).

Conclusion

We can compare the evidence for textual integrity for both the New Testament and the Qur'an. We find that the oldest surviving texts of the Qur'an, whether in sizeable fragments or whole, originate not earlier than about one and a half centuries after Muhammad's death. As for the Old Testament, evidence is available for texts dating from before the time of Jesus. Concerning the New Testament, there are a few fragments which may be 1st century, many other fragments date from the early part of the 2nd century and almost complete texts from the end of that century. In other words, the interval between composition and the first texts of the Qur'an appears to be about 150 years. For the New Testament, the interval is between 40 and 125.

Both the Bible and Qur'an have suffered from variant readings. In the case of the Qur'an, variants were officially suppressed and the study of them nowadays is not encouraged in Islamic circles. In the case of the Bible, the Church has not found it necessary to favour one variant while suppressing all others. A summary of textual variations in the Bible can be found in most modern Bible translations, and research studies are also available. In the case of the Qur'an, such a facility is not available in any of the current editions and commentaries on the Qur'an. One has to go back almost a thousand years to classical writings (mostly in Arabic and Farsi) on the Qur'anic science of compilation and commentary to find discussions on some although not all variations in the Qur'an.

4

The Qur'anic testimony

Six centuries after Jesus, the Qur'an gave unequivocal confirmation of both the Jewish and the Christian Scriptures. The Qur'an states that one reason for its being revealed was so that the Arabs would not make the excuse that the Scriptures were sent down only to Jews and Christians (Surah 6:156–157). The Qur'an was sent to establish a law for the Arabs that was substantially the same as that which God sent to Abraham, Moses and Jesus in order that they too might be guided on to the straight path (Surah 42:13). The Qur'an, as available today, instructs Muslims to believe in what was revealed to Muhammad but also to believe in 'the Scriptures which He sent to those before him' (Surah 4:136).

Yet the only Scriptures mentioned by name in the Qur'an, apart from two early references to the *Suhuf* (scrolls) of Abraham and Moses (87:19; 53:36–37), are the Tawrat of Moses, the Zabur of David and the Injil of Jesus. These titles are still used by Christians and Jews, that is, by those called 'the people of the book' by the Qur'an. Tawrat is the Hebrew Torah, meaning the books containing 'instructions', the term which came to be used among the Jews as the technical term for the law and, by extension, for the law embodied in the whole collection known today also as the Old Testament.

Similarly *'Zabur'* is an Arabicized form of the Hebrew word *'Mizmor'* while *'Injil'* is from the Greek word *'evangelion'*. The word passed into Arabic through the Ethiopic *Wangel*[1] as used by Christians in Syria, Egypt and around Arabia to identify the four narratives of the Gospel together with other books known today as the New Testament.

The Tawrat

The Qur'an makes clear that it was God who sent the Tawrat to the Israelites (Surah 3:3; 45:16; 40:53; 2:41). It is described as a light and a warning to the God-fearing people (Surah 21:48 cf. 40:54). It is called an *Imam*, a leader (Surah 11:17–20), a guide and a mercy (Surah 6:154). The list of references is very long. The Qur'an claims that after Moses, the Tawrat was inherited by the prophets of Israel, who judged the people according to its laws (Surah 5:44). Mary the mother of Jesus is commended as believing in it (Surah 66:12). Similarly God commanded John the Baptist (known as Yahyah in the Qur'an) to follow it (Surah 3:48). Later God taught the Tawrat to Jesus who later came to confirm it (Surah 61:6; 3:50). It was read and studied by his contemporaries (Surah 3:79). Later still it was inherited by the teachers of the Jews (Surah 5:44). Finally it came down to the Jews of Arabia, Muhammad's contemporaries, who had copies which he asked them to bring out and read. The Qur'an further tells us that the Jews around Muhammad in Madina studied it, believing that it was something revealed from the Lord (Surah 2:44; 5:43; 7:169).

---

[1] Arthur Jeffery, *Foreign Vocabulary of the Qur'an*, p.71.

The Zabur

The Zabur was the book given to David (Surah 4:163; 17:55), 'a blessed book sent down to him' (Surah 38:29). God gave him the gift of the Scripture, wisdom and prophecy, because he was one of Abraham's rightly guided descendants (Surah 6:84).

Yusuf Ali, in his commentary on the Qur'an, declares the Zabur to be a spiritual gift from God. He states, 'David was given the Zabur, the Psalter or Psalms, intended [then] to be sung for the worship of Allah and the celebration of Allah's praise.'[2] In his view, David's Psalms are still extant 'though their present form may possibly be different from the original' and though they include 'Psalms not written by David,' they still 'contain much devotional poetry of a high order.'[3]

The Qur'an has its own way of retelling the narratives of the prophets and people mentioned in the Bible, but interestingly it has one direct quote from the Psalms, stating, 'Before this we wrote in the Psalms after the message (given to Moses): "My servants, the righteous shall inherit the earth" ' (Surah 21:105; Psalm 37:29).

The Injil

According to the Qur'an the Injil was the revelation given to Jesus, who was taught by God (Surah 3:48; 57:27; 5:46). It was revealed, just as other Scriptures were (Surah 3:65; 5:47), and contains direction, guidance and light (Surah 5:46; 3:3). God also inspired the disciples of Jesus. They believed what was revealed to Jesus and to them (Surah

---

[2] Yusuf Ali, *The Meaning of the Holy Qur'an*, p.689, note 2241.
[3] Yusuf Ali, p.238, note 669.

5:111; 3:53). In Muhammad's time, this collection was available to Christians who were advised to follow it and judge according to it (Surah 5:47).

The theory of corruption

Say ye: We believe in Allah, and the revelation given to us, and to Abraham, Isma'il, Isaac, Jacob, and the tribes, and that given to Moses and Jesus, and that given to (all) prophets from their Lord: We make no difference between one and another of them: and we submit to Allah. (Surah 2:136)[4]

The Qur'an asks Muslims to confirm their faith in the above words. However, despite such instructions, many Muslims today *do* differentiate; not only between Muhammad and other prophets, but also between the Qur'an and the Bible. Most maintain that the Bible has been corrupted, while the Qur'an is 'perfectly preserved and protected from human tampering'.[5] A Muslim apologist, Ajijolah, for example, asserts, 'The fact is that the original Word of God is preserved neither with the Jews nor with the Christians. The Qur'an on the other hand, is fully preserved and not a jot or tittle has been changed or left out.'[6]

The testimony of the Qur'an itself refutes the notion of corruption. It claims to testify to the truth of previous Scriptures but also puts them side by side with itself by saying that those who reject these books will be punished (Surah 35:25,26; Surah 40:70,71).

Mary, the mother of Jesus, is said in the Qur'an to have believed in the words of God and his books (Surah 66:12).

---

[4] Yusuf Ali, *The Holy Qur'an: English translation of the meanings and commentary*, p.54.
[5] Deedat, *Is the Bible God's Word?*, p.7.
[6] Ajijola, *The Essence of Faith in Islam*, p.79.

Since the Qur'an says that Mary believed in God's books, *Kutubihi*, this presumably refers to all the books; the Torah, the Psalms, the books of the prophets. Surely Muslims will agree that God would have warned her if the books had been corrupted.

From the Qur'an it is also obvious that the Torah existed in its true form at the time of Jesus, and that the Jews read it. Otherwise his contemporary John the Baptist would not have been admonished by God to follow it (Surah 19:12). God would not have asked him 'to take hold of the Book' if there was the slightest doubt of its corruption or any chance of alteration in it.

The Qur'an says that God taught Jesus the Torah and the Gospel (Surah 3:48; 5:113). Jesus, during his preaching and teaching, testified and attested to the truth of the Torah (Surah 3:49–50; 61:6). The Qur'an further states that the Gospel confirms the truth of the Torah (Surah 5:49). From all this one can conclude that the books of both Jews and Christians, before and at the time of Muhammad, were in existence in a reliable form and also that Jews and Christians were reading, studying and teaching these books.

Further, the Qur'an calls Jews and Christians 'People of the Scripture', *ahl al kitab* (Surah 2:44,113,121; 3:78,79; 5:43; 6:92; 7:157; 10:95). This title also demonstrates that the Scriptures from which these two communities received their title were in their possession and were in use for the spiritual and social regulation of their lives.

The Qur'an testifies that its main purpose is to provide a revelation for Arabic speaking people, who could not understand (or did not have access to) the Scriptures of the Jews and Christians (Surah 46:11–12; 41:2–3; 20:112; 39:29; 12:2). There is no suggestion that this new revelation (the Qur'an) was needed to *replace* any corrupted Scripture. In fact, the Qur'an claimed to be a *verification* of the earlier revelations such as in the Torah and the Gospel, that went before it (Surah 10:37; 12:111).

Charges against the People of the Book

Those who raise the accusation of corruption in the Bible ignore the many translations of it which already existed long before the rise of Islam; the Septuagint in Egypt, the Syriac and the Vulgate. If discrepancies in these had affected the divine teaching of the Scriptures, the prophet of Islam, being inspired by God (as Muslims believe) would surely never have commended them as he did, nor enjoined their observance on the Jews and Christians in these words:

> Let the People of the Gospel judge by what Allah hath revealed therein. If any do fail to judge by (the light of) what Allah hath revealed, they are (no better than) those who rebel (Surah 5:47).

> Say: O People of the Book! Ye have no ground to stand upon unless ye stand fast by the Law, the Gospel, and all the revelation that has come to you from your Lord (Surah 5:68).

Had the earlier Scriptures not been genuine and accurate before and during the time of Muhammad, then the Qur'an would not have instructed the Jews and Christians to follow that which had been revealed in their Scriptures.

Some Muslims say that the pre-Islamic Scriptures were changed sometime after Muhammad began preaching, or *after* Islam had spread into other parts of the world. This hypothesis, however, would not only contradict the documentary evidence but would also contradict the Qur'an.

Since it claims to be the guardian of the previous Scriptures, therefore any Muslim who claims that there has been corruption of the text of the Torah and the Injil also, inevitably, charges the Qur'an with failure in its role in 'guarding' them (Surah 5:48). The Arabic word is *muhaimena*, watcher over it. Qadhi Nasiruddin Abusaeed Al-Baidhawi (d.1286) in his commentary, *Anwar al-Tanzeel*, expounds this verse saying that the Qur'an is the protector of all sacred books, to preserve them from any kind of change.[7]

It is also important to note that the Qur'an does not say that Jews and Christians are reciters or readers of false Scriptures. While it does accuse some of the Jews of corrupting, changing, mispronouncing and concealing the words of God when reading them aloud, nowhere does it claim that the actual text of the previous Scriptures is corrupted in such a way that they should not be believed and read.

We do note, however, from some verses of the Qur'an that it appears that some Jews around Muhammad in Madinah concealed some texts and mingled the truth with falsehood (for example Surah 2:40–42; 2:75–79; 2:101,140, 2:156,159,174; 3:70–72, 78,187; 4:46; 5:41; 7:162). When looked at in context, however, most of the charges directed against the Jews of Madinah as mentioned in the Qur'an, imply that the Jews misinterpreted or corrupted what *Muhammad* had said.

Just as the Qur'an denounces the Jews, so the Bible is also filled with denunciations of the sins and apostasy of the Israelites. Had tampering by the Jews been possible, such passages in the Bible would surely have been the first to be altered by them, as well as the prophecies about Jesus.

---

[7] Baidhawi, *Commentarius in Coranum*, Vol 1. p.260.

The Qur'anic words

In several places in the Qur'an, the dishonesty or bad behaviour of the Jews is denounced using the words *tahrif*, to corrupt, *lawa*, to twist, *kitman*, to conceal and *tabdil*, to change. Nowhere, are these words used against Christians. Presumably, most of these passages refer to Muhammad's contacts with his Jewish contemporaries who knew their Scriptures in Hebrew and translated portions for him into Arabic. It seems as though some of them deliberately altered words in order to deceive or mock the prophet.[8] The Jews were consequently accused of hiding the truth. There are only four verses in the Qur'an where some and not all Jews are accused of *altering words* (Surah 2:75; 4:46; 5:13,41).

In addition to these verses, in some places the Jews are also accused of *twisting their tongues* i.e. deliberately mispronouncing words and concealing some verses when they read their Scriptures. One of the traditions states that when some Jewish rabbis were asked about something in the Torah, they concealed it and refused to say anything about it. So God sent down a revelation about them in the following words, 'Those who conceal, *yaktumuna*, the clear (signs) We have sent down and guidance, after We have made it clear for the People in the Book – on them shall be Allah's curse . . .' (Surah 2:159).[9]

In another place the Qur'an admonishes some of the Jews because they 'change the words from their (right) times and places' (Surah 5:41). Ar-Razi takes the perversion to mean the denial of certain truths in their books, not the changing of the text. This Qur'anic passage

---

[8] Arthur Jeffery, *The Qur'an as Scripture*, pp 72f.

[9] Ibn Hisham, *Sira* (trans.), Guilliam, *The Life of Muhammad*, p.250.

refers to the case of a couple from Khyber caught in adultery. The tradition is that, to pass a judgement according to the Torah, Muhammad asked a rabbi to read the relevant passage. The rabbi hid the passage of stoning in the Torah and started reading somewhere else. Abdullah b. Salam struck the rabbi's hand saying, 'This, O prophet of God, is the verse of stoning which he refuses to read to you.' Muhammad then said, 'Woe to you Jews! What has induced you to abandon the judgement of God which you hold in your hands?'[10] The Bible passage that prescribes stoning as the penalty for adultery was then (and still is) available in the Bible (Deuteronomy 22:22–27). Some Jews around Muhammad may have concealed these verses but they did not remove them from the text.

At another place, the Qur'an castigated the Jews of Madinah saying, 'There is among them a section who distort the Book with their tongues: (as they read) you would think it is a part of the Book, but it is not part of the Book ...' (Surah 3:78 also in 4:46). Here the technical word *lawa* is used, which would suggest that they mispronounced words by 'distorting their tongues'. There is no suggestion that the text was distorted in its written form.

Muslim traditions giving the reason and background (*Asbab an-nazul*) of certain passages of the Qur'an indicate that *some* Jews were accused, not of changing their own Scriptures, but of altering and distorting the verses of the Qur'an which Muhammad had transmitted (Surah 2:75–79; 4:44–47; 5:44–51). This would mean that this charge of corruption is therefore made not against *all* Jews but only those who misquoted the words of the Qur'an or of Muhammad.

---

[10] Ibn Hisham, *Sira*, p.267.

The opinion of some prominent Muslims

The available documentary evidence, concerning the life of the first Muslim community, shows that the standards used by modern Muslims to demonstrate corruption in the earlier Scriptures, were alien to the first followers of Islam. A great number of traditions (*Ahadith*) refer to Muhammad asking for the Torah when he was asked to judge some disputes, and having it read aloud to him (see Chapter 5). These traditions strongly imply that the Torah present in the seventh century in Arabia was considered to be uncorrupted.

There is one tradition in *Sahih al-Bukhari* which may imply corruption. It quotes Abdullah ibn Abbas (d.687 CE), one of the most celebrated of the companions of Muhammad, and the relater of numerous traditions (although he was only thirteen years old at the time of Muhammad's death).[11] He said, 'People of the Scriptures have changed some of Allah's books and distorted them and written something with their own hands . . .'[12] It is important to note, however, that Ibn Abbas' view in regard to *tahrif* was of an interpretation. For example, he is recorded as having said: 'there is no man who could corrupt a single word of what proceeds from God, so that the Jews and Christians could corrupt only by misrepresenting the *meaning* of the words of God.'[13]

Although the majority of Muslims nowadays cling to a less favourable view of the Bible, there have been and still are some Muslims who hold the view that the Bible has not been corrupted. In line with the teaching of the Qur'an, they refuse to entertain the possibility of

[10] Ibn Hisham, *Sira*, p.267.
[11] Muhammad Zubayr Siddiqi, *Hadith Literature*, p.21.
[12] *Sahih Al-Bukhari*, Vol. 6, p.461.
[13] Hughes, *Dictionary of Islam*, p.62.

corruption in the earlier Scriptures. In their opinion, if the prophet Muhammad himself was cautioned not to doubt the books of Moses (Surah 32:24), then they also have no right or justification to doubt the veracity of the earlier Scriptures, especially if they wish to follow the *Sunnah*, the example of the prophet.

Imam Fakhr al-Din Razi (d.1210 CE) believed that *tahrif* referred to meaning, not to the text. He believed that textual falsification was improbable.[14] Jalaluddin Suyuti (d.1500), in his *Tafsir Durr al-Mansur*, quotes Ibn Mazar and Abi Hatim 'that they have it on the authority of Ibn Muniyah that the Tawrat and Injil are in the same state of purity in which they were sent down from heaven and that no alteration had been made in them, but that the Jews were wont to deceive the people by unsound arguments, and by wresting the sense of the Scripture.'[15] Shah Wali Allah (d.1762 CE), 'the most prominent Muslim intellectual of eighteenth century India and a prolific writer,'[16] in his famous Persian work *Al-Fawz al-Kabir fi usul al-tafsir* supports this same view.[17]

These examples show that the references in the Qur'an that speak of corruption do not refer to any act beyond that of the obstructive behaviour of some Jews, their wrong interpretations and use of the Scriptures. To say otherwise goes beyond the actual meaning of the Qur'an.

---

[14] Razi (See for example comments on Surah 5:13 in his *Mufatih al-Ghaib aw al-tafsir al-Kabir*, Vol. 5, p.187 Cairo: 1933).

[15] Hughes, *Dictionary of Islam*, p.62.

[16] Hermansen, 'Shah Wali Allah', in *The Oxford Encyclopaedia of the Modern Islamic World*, Vol. 4, p.311.

[17] Hughes, *Dictionary of Islam*, p.62.

Differing views

One may ask why, then, there are Muslims who believe in the textual corruption of the Bible. When Muslims first came out of Arabia, and mixed with the people of the Book, they found that their Scriptures were different from the Qur'an in terms of some material facts and doctrines. As time passed, Muslim historians, polemicists and apologists reacted to the differences in various ways, but almost all alleged that the people of the Book had introduced some form of corruption. Some stayed with the original opinion of *tahrif bi'al Ma'ni*, corruption in the meaning, but others went further with the idea of *tahrif bi'al lafz*, textual alteration.

The latter idea gained greater popularity among ordinary Muslim believers. Some rejected the Bible totally, while others accepted that it contained elements of the original Gospel. To accommodate the Qur'anic statement, 'No one can change the word of God', with their idea of *tahrif bi'al lafz*, some nowadays suggest that corruption only occurred in the narratives and not in the direct speech of God or prophet as reported in the Bible.[18] Both the Qur'an and the previous Scriptures are contradicted in equal measure by this view, as will be shown in the following chapters.

Every Muslim scholar approaches the diversity of opinion regarding the Bible in a different manner. Some use the Bible to support their own particular view of Islam and Christianity. Others reject the Bible totally but still use it to prove some point. This, again, is not new. Many Muslim scholars from the ninth century onward, have written polemical refutations of Christianity. It seems that, from that date on, a split started to take place among Muslims

---

[18] Mawdudi, *Tafhim ul-Qur'an*, Vol.1, p.231–232.

on the question of *tahrif*. The dominant view gradually became the accusation *tahrif bi'al lafz* that the text itself had been corrupted. The Spanish theologians Ibn Hazm (d.1064) and Al-Biruni (d.1050), along with most Muslims, upheld this view. Ibn Hazm in his book, *Kitab al-fisal fil-milal wal-ihawa'wal-nihal* listed many contradictions in the Bible that he thought significant.[19] He followed a literal interpretation of the Qur'an and, given the obvious contradictions between the Qur'an and the Gospel accounts regarding Jesus, he chose to believe that there had been corruption of the text in both the Jewish and Christian Scriptures. He did not base his argument on historical facts, but rather on his own assumptions, that is, to safeguard his own way of understanding the words of the Qur'an. His studies led him to issue a full-fledged accusation of corruption in the previous Scriptures, *tahrif bi'al lafz*. His study to prove the falsification of the Bible takes up the whole of the second volume of his book. He went so far as to claim, 'the Gospels are the work of accursed liars.'[20] Some may feel offended by the curses and abusive language in this book. Although there are few disciples among Muslims following his *Zahiri*, literalistic exegesis of the Qur'an and traditions, his style and methods in the field of anti-Christian polemics have been borrowed by many Muslim writers.

Some of the present day writers and commentators want to hold to both opinions: They assert that the Bible is corrupted (where they disagree with it) but not to the extent that it can be discarded totally i.e., they cite from those parts which they do agree with. For example Rashid Rida, commenting on the Jewish Scriptures,

---

[19] *Kitab al-fisal fil-milal wal-ihawa'wal-nihal*, Vol. 1 & 2 (Dar ul-jil, Beirut, 1985).

[20] Ibn Hazm, *Kitab al-fisal fil-milal wal-ihawa'wal-nihal*, Vol. 2, p.21.

says that 'the substance of their religion, *jawahir dinihim,* has remained recognisable, not distorted to the extent that guidance from its precepts is completely blocked.'[21]

Some scholars who stand for the idea of *tahrif bi'al lafz* refer to the writings known as the *apocrypha* that were around in the time of Muhammad. For example, Kamil Hussain suggests that the Qur'an speaking of corruption means the *apocrypha* writings that were available in the Near-East at that time but are not recognised as authentic by the Christians of our time.[22]

In spite of such varying ideas, there have been other Muslim theologians who thought otherwise: some of them are respected scholars in Islamics, some are commentators of the Qur'an and others historians. To harmonise the verses of the Qur'an that speak of the earlier Scriptures as guidance and light, such scholars adopted the view that alteration took place in meaning, *tahrif bi'al ma'ni,* without tampering with the text itself. In spite of hard-line opposition, there are several modern Muslim thinkers and theologians who have added their names to the list of earlier Muslims like Ibn Khaldun, Ar-Razi and Al-Ghazzali and several others who honoured the integrity of the text of the Bible – men such as Syed Ahmad Khan, Mawlawi Chiragh ud Din, Mawlawi Muhammad Sa'id, Sayyid Ahmad Husayn Shawkat Mirthi, the Egyptian scholar Muhammad Abduh[23], Ghulam Jilani Burq.[24]

---

[21] Rashid Rida, *Tafsir al-Manar*, Vol 1, p.337.

[22] Kamil Hussain, *Al-Dhikr al-Hakim*, pp.106–108, (Cairo: 1972).

[23] Yusaf Jalil, *The Authenticity of Scriptures*, Al-Mushir, (Urdu) Rawalpindi: 1976, pp.49–51.

[24] Burq, *Do Islam*, pp.191–200.

Conclusion

Although Muslim theologians are divided on the question of the integrity of the Christian Scriptures, the Qur'anic testimony itself is quite clear. It affirms the reliability of the Bible. Furthermore, the Qur'an clearly suggests that the Torah was available to the prophets who came after Moses. Additionally, the Qur'an suggests that other books like the Psalms, and books of the prophets, were also available e.g. to God's people such as Mary, John the Baptist, Jesus and his first-century disciples.

At the time of Muhammad, there were true Christians and Jews whose faith is commended in some passages of the Qur'an. We learn from the Qur'an and available traditions that the Scriptures were available in a trustworthy form. Muhammad claimed that since the Arabs did not understand the language of the earlier Scriptures, God now revealed the Qur'an to Muhammad for such Arabs.

The Qur'an refers to the *Torah* and the *Injil* more than a hundred times. There are about twenty occurrences where they are mentioned by name. On occasions when Muhammad wanted to settle a dispute with or between the Jews of Madinah, he would ask for the Torah to be brought and read, a fact which shows that he trusted it. He accused some of the Jews of *tahrif bi-al ma'ni* because they concealed or misquoted their own Scriptures and the Qur'an.

The Qur'an says that no one can change the Word of God. If the Jews did corrupt the Word of God then it would mean that the Qur'anic statement is unreliable, a concept that would be blasphemy to Muslims. The only possible conclusion in the light of the Qur'an is therefore that the copies of the pre-Islamic Scriptures (known as the Torah and the Injil) were available in the days of Muhammad as they are available today i.e. that they *are* valid. Since Christians have ample documentary evidence from before Muhammad's time, they can confidently assert that their Scriptures are trustworthy.

5

Errors and contradictions?

'How can you believe a Bible that is full of contradictions and errors and has many versions?' This question is asked very often by Muslims in conversation with Christians. It presupposes that the Bible is riddled with so many discrepancies that it is impossible to believe in its integrity. It is asserted that the writers were not inspired; if they had been, they would not have committed historical and scientific blunders. Neither would there have been copyists' errors nor would it have contained contradictory teachings. It is these inconsistencies and discrepancies which, they believe, destroy the credibility of the biblical Scriptures.

Christians respond that the actual number of copyists' errors in the manuscripts (as Muslims and other critics call them) are minimal, especially when compared with non-biblical manuscripts of similar antiquity. Christians disagree with the premise that their Scriptures are full of contradictions and errors. Just as there are critics of the Qur'an who say that Qur'anic verses lack consistency, coherence and are in many respects contradictory, so there are critics of the Bible who have raised the same objections against the Bible, saying that the Christian Scriptures contain only the compositions of people who were not inspired. Defenders of the Qur'an claim that there are answers and reasons available concerning each verse in the Qur'an that critics have described as inconsistent and incoherent. Similarly, defenders of the Bible have answers and reasons for the alleged errors and contradictions found in the Bible. In fact, we find that both sides are willing to admit that their Scriptures contain certain passages which may be unclear (*Mutashabihat*) and indeed, that some may even appear to be contradictory. In this chapter, we survey most, but not all, of the important accusations of *errors* and *inaccuracies* that are commonly pointed out by Muslims in their discussion with Christians, and in their writings. We will also see if there is a Christian response to these accusations.

Historical errors in the Bible

Some Muslim writers assert that parts of the Bible have historical errors. Most of their objections are similar to those raised in the 18th and 19th century by secular historians and textual critics. Although new evidence disproves these 'historical errors', somehow Muslims still use them to 'disparage' the integrity of the Bible. More than any other books in the New Testament, we find that the Gospel according to Luke and the Acts of the Apostles speak of specific people and places. These details gave critics opportunities to question the historicity of these two books; and Muslim critics have also joined this debate. Now, however, the accounts in Luke and Acts of the Apostles are being vindicated by new findings in archaeology, or from rediscovered ancient texts.

For example according to Luke, John the Baptist began his ministry when Lysanias was district ruler of Abilene (Luke 3:1). Following some Western critics, Muslims also questioned this statement because Josephus in his writings mentioned a Lysanias who ruled Abilene and died in 34 BCE i.e. long before the birth of John the Baptist.[1] Archaeologists have now uncovered an inscription in Abilene mentioning another Lysanias who was tetrarch (district ruler) during the reign of Tiberius Caesar, i.e. at the same time as John began his ministry.[2]

Another instance is Quirinius, whom Luke described as the governor of Syria at the time of the birth of Jesus (Luke 2:1–3). Luke also records the taking of a census. Following Western critics, Muslim writers have questioned both statements.[3] However, it has now been discovered that the Romans made regular enrolments of taxpayers and also held a census every 14 years. It has also been found that Quirinius was indeed governor of Syria around 7 BCE.[4]

Luke's references to places and incidents are now believed by critics to be accurate. For example, Luke summarises Paul's address to the people of Athens by saying that he had observed an altar that was dedicated 'to an unknown God' (Acts 17:23). Altars dedicated to anonymous gods have indeed been discovered in other parts of the territory of the Roman Empire. One was found in Pergamum with the inscription written in Greek, just as would have been the case in Athens.

Luke's terminology was again criticised in that he was not thought to be technically correct to call the civil ruler of Thessalonica a *Politarch* (Acts 17:6). In fact, nineteen inscriptions have come to light that make use of this title, five of which are in particular reference to Thessalonica. Luke's usage of *Praetor* to describe the Philippian ruler

---

[1] Rahmatullah, *Izharul Haqq*, Part 2, p.120.
[2] *The New International Dictionary of Biblical Archaeology*, p.294. Ed. 1983.
[3] Rahmatullah, *Izharul Haqq*, Part 2, p.119.
[4] Werner Keller, *The Bible as History*, p.344.

(instead of the term *Duumuris*) was once thought to be inaccurate but has also been found to be correct. Similarly his usage of the word 'Proconsul' as the title for Gallio (Acts 18:12) is correct as corroborated by the Delphi inscription (52 CE) which states in part: 'As Lucius Junius Gallio, my friend and the Proconsul of Achaia . . .'. Interestingly Gallio held this position for only one year, suggesting that the writer of the Acts of the Apostles accurately describes the situation in or around 52 CE, the year in question.

In the 1960s the name of the Roman governor, Pontius Pilate, was found on an inscription from the ruins of a Roman theatre at Caesarea.[5] Until this discovery, there had been frequent questions about the existence of this particular Roman ruler among the harsher critics of the Bible. Now, one can comfortably state that no archaeological discovery has contradicted a biblical reference to the extent that it implies that the Bible cannot be trusted. More and more people are coming to recognise the value of biblical information, largely in response to the increasing number of discoveries from archaeological excavations.

Examples of Qur'anic historical errors

It is interesting to note that, while some Muslims find alleged historical *mistakes* in the Bible, it is easy to point to several mistakes in the Qur'an. For example:

1. Abraham's father's name was Terah (Genesis 11:26; 1 Chronicles 1:26) but the Qur'an says it was Azar (Surah 6:74). According to the Bible, a man with a similar name, Eliezer, was Abraham's servant (Genesis 15:2–3).

---

[5] *Biblical Archaeological Review*, May/June 1982, p30,31.

2. The Qur'an speaks of Mary, the mother of Jesus as Aaron's sister (Surah 19:28), confusing her with the sister of Aaron with the same name, who lived about 1600 years before the mother of Jesus (Exodus 15:20).

3. Haman is mentioned as Pharaoh's minister (Surah 28:6,8). The actual Haman lived a thousand years after Pharaoh in Babylon (Esther 3:1).

4. Relating the story of Moses, the Qur'an states that while Moses was away, a Samaritan fashioned a golden calf for the Israelites (Surah 20:85). In fact, Samaritans as a named group existed only after the Israelite captivity in Babylon, that is, several centuries after Moses (1 Kings 16:24).

Some Muslim exegetes have tried to solve these *errors* in much the same way as Christians have done in the case of the Bible (which is not the issue here). Surely the crux of the matter is that if such examples do not affect the integrity of the Qur'an, then is it right for a Muslim to criticise the Bible by using a different yardstick in the case of the Bible to that used for the Qur'an?

Numerical discrepancies in the Bible

In their criticisms, some Muslims refer to numerical contradictions in the Bible, many of which can be settled by considering the context and the time when the passages of Scripture were first written. For other passages one has to agree to a scribal mistake. In ancient times, Hebrew letters were used for numbers, so mistakes in numbers, especially when the numeral letters were blurred or unskilfully written, would be inevitable. Such numerical discrepancies do not alter any vital point of Scripture. However, to discredit the Bible, some Muslims have presumed to make mock, saying, 'The God of the Bible is weak in mathematics.'[6]

Noah's age?

Muslims point out that in Genesis 6:3 God sets a limit to man's life span of one hundred and twenty years but two chapters later the Bible states that Noah died at the age of nine hundred and fifty (Genesis 9:29).[7] Christians usually respond by saying that either God meant a *respite* of one hundred and twenty years before the flood, or that human life should gradually diminish to that length. Reformers like Luther and Calvin upheld the idea that one hundred and twenty years indicated the grace period, after which the flood came. However, Muslims argue that such an interpretation cannot be right because Noah should have been six hundred and twenty years old at the time of the flood, but the Bible states that he was six hundred years old (Genesis 7:6; 5:32).[8]

A Christian response to this issue is that the Bible has perhaps used a 'rounded' figure. The use of approximate or rounded off numbers is a common practice among Muslims as well. For instance, according to Ibn Abbas, Muhammad 'started receiving the divine inspiration at the age of forty. Then he stayed in Mecca for thirteen years, receiving the Divine revelation. Then he was ordered to migrate and he lived as an emigrant for ten years, and then died at the age of sixty three.'[9]

---

[6] Bashir Ansari, *Bible main tahrif ke matni Saboot*, p.9.
[7] Baggil, *Christian Muslim Dialogue*, p.12.
[8] Baggil, *Christian Muslim Dialogue*, p.12.
[9] *Sahih al-Bukhari*, Vol 5, p.242.

However at another place he says, 'The Prophet stayed for ten years in Mecca with the Qur'an being revealed to him and he stayed in Madina for ten years.'[10] Similarly while Ibn Abbas and Aisha say that Muhammad died at the age of sixty three, Anas Ibn Malik says the Prophet died 'when he was sixty'.[11]

Noah's ark

Some Muslims find a contradiction between Genesis 6:19,20 and Genesis 7:8,9. They argue that God first tells Noah to bring into the ark two of all living creatures but a few verses later changes his mind and asks Noah to take seven of every kind of clean animal and two of every kind of unclean animal, and also seven pairs of every kind of bird.[12]

The first passage is a general command in which no clean or unclean animals are specified. In the later statement God amplified and explained further to Noah to take with him seven pairs of clean animals and birds both for breeding and sacrifices. In Genesis 8:20 it is said about Noah that, after the flood, when he came out together with his family and all the other creatures, he built an altar to the Lord. He took some of all the clean animals and clean birds and sacrificed them there (Genesis 8:18–20).

Perhaps the simplest explanation is to suppose that the first passage simply asserts that the animals and birds should come *paired*; the second however specifies the *number* of the pairs, seven pairs of the clean and two pairs of the unclean animals.

---

[10]   *Sahih al-Bukhari*, Vol.5, p.156.

[11]   *Sahih al-Bukhari*, Vol 5, p.528; *Muwatta Imam Malik*, p.384.

[12]   Rahmatullah, *Izharul Haqq*, Part 2, p.5.

Solomon's military might

Some scholars refer to passages like 2 Chronicles 9:25 and 1 Kings 4:26 as contradictory. The first passage says that Solomon had 40,000 stalls of horses for his chariots and 12,000 horsemen. The latter says that Solomon had 4,000 stalls for horses and chariots and twelve thousand horsemen.[13]

It may simply be that the number of stalls recorded in one was the number at the beginning of Solomon's reign, whereas the other was the number at its end. Solomon reigned for 40 years, so the size of the military establishment his father had had increased or decreased during that time.

Another example of apparent contradiction is from 1 Kings 5:16 and 2 Chronicles 2:2. Objectors reason that one passage has the number of Solomon's officers who looked after his work as 3,300 while the other passage the number who oversee the work is 3,600.

Commentators have suggested that the extra 300 in 2 Chronicles were men held in reserve i.e. to take the place of any who became ill or died. Thus in one passage it is the basic supervisory force that is numbered whereas in the other the replacements are included within the total. This explanation makes sense and is consistent with Solomon's wisdom.

Numerical contradictions are found in the Qur'an as well. For example, in a number of verses of the Qur'an, it is stated that the earth and the heavens were created in six days (Surah 7:54; 10:3; 25:59; 50:38), yet in another place the number of days is increased (Surah 41:9–12). Counting the number of days in this passage, the impression is that it took eight and not six days. At one place in the Qur'an it is stated that a day with Allah is equal to a thousand years

---

[13] Rahmatullah, *Izharul Haqq*, Part 2, p.9.

(Surah 32:5), yet another passage equals it to 50,000 years (Surah 70:4).

Muslims have ways of explaining these discrepancies, just as Christians do in the case of the Bible. This is not the point in this case; rather, if such discrepancies do not effect the status of the Qur'an then they are not harmful to the integrity of the Bible either.

Variants of the biblical text

In several places in the Bible, we find that the passage may have a variant reading. Information on such a reading is usually found in the footnotes or in the page margin. For example, in the English translation of the Bible known as the New International Version (NIV), a footnote might state with the words, 'Many early manuscripts . . .'; 'Some manuscripts . . .' or 'Some early manuscripts . . .' etc.

Some Muslims draw attention to these variant readings to discredit the authenticity of the whole Bible. As a practical demonstration during a discussion, a Muslim will show copies of the Qur'an or ask several Muslim friends to recite a portion of it (by heart or from their copies) to claim that there are no textual variants for the Qur'an as there are for the Bible.

However, as we have seen already, while there are two versions of the Qur'an, the *Warsh* and the *Hafsh* which have a few minor diacritical variants, there were many variants of the Qur'an in circulation prior to its being standardised. Some Muslim scholars now admit this fact and thus follow Abdur Rahman Doi's words, that the Qur'an's 'new version must have gradually driven out the variants because of its official authority and the general desire for uniformity.'[14]

---

[14] Abdur Rahman Doi, *Qur'an: An Introduction*, p.27.

Here are a few examples of variants which any Muslim with even a passing acquaintance with the Qur'an will recognise easily:

In the present text of the Qur'an one reads, *Thalikal Kitaabu laa rayba fiih*, 'This is the Scripture of which there is no doubt' (Surah 2:1). Ibn Masood's text, along with several others, stated: *Tanziilul Kitabu laa rayba fiih*, '[This is] the Scripture sent down of which there is no doubt.'

In verse 198 of Surah 2, Masood included the extra phrase, *fi Mawasemel hajj* (in the season of pilgrimage) after *an tabteghu fadhlen merrabekum* (you seek the bounty of your Lord). Similarly, in the present Qur'an, Surah 3:19 reads, *Innaddina inddallaahil islamm*, the religion before God is Islam, but Ibn Masood's text had the word *al-Hanifiyya*, (the true way) instead of the word *Islam*.

In Surah 3 the last part of verse 43 reads, *wasjudi warkai ma-arrke-ein*, 'prostrate thyself and bow with those who bow [in worship]', but Ibn Masood's reading was, *warkai wasjudi fes-sajedeen*, 'bow thyself and prostrate among those who prostrate.'[15]

One could go on and on to state many more of these variants. If the variants that were extant before the present version of the Qur'an do not destroy the integrity of the Qur'anic text, then the same is true in the case of the Bible.

Missing and omitted verses

In discussions to 'prove' that the Bible has grave defects, the examples of John 8:1–11 and Mark 16:9–20 are often the first to be cited.[16] Muslims argue that since these passages are included in the King James Version but are

---

[15] *Kitab al-Masahif.*

[16] Ulfat Aziz-us-Samad, *A Comparative Study of Christianity and Islam*, p.4.

Figure 12. An example of variants in Surah al-Asr

1. The Surah as it appears in today's Qur'an.   2. Ali Ibn Abi Talib's
reading of the same Surah.   3 & 4. Readings attributed to Ibn Masud.
(Source: Kitab al- Masahif, pp. 192, 111, 55)

excluded from the main text of the 'Revised Standard Version', being relegated to footnotes only, such treatment is
obviously proof that Christians have corrupted their
Scriptures.[17]

Christians respond that the King James and Revised
Versions are *translations* and that the translators have not
corrupted the text but have only provided their own view
of the facts. Although some ancient manuscripts do not
contain these 'additional texts', they are nevertheless
found in other manuscripts e.g. where John 8:1–11 is
placed after 7:36 or 21:25 or even Luke 21:38. Mark's

---

[17] Bilal Philips, *The True Message of Jesus Christ*, p.14.

passage is included in the Alexandrian, Old Syriac and Latin codices. Irenaeus (d.200) referred to it in his writing. In any case, both passages are not lost because they are still available. This response from Christians does not often satisfy the objectors who continue to insist that, as some ancient manuscripts do not contain these verses, the Bible is clearly not authentic. Unfortunately, the same Muslims also ignore the fact that Qur'anic manuscripts from the companions of Muhammad had similar problems. Ibn Masood's manuscript did not include the first and the two last of the chapters of the present Qur'an. Muslim scholars state that he did not consider them part of the Qur'anic Scripture.

To 'prove' the corruption of the Bible, Muslims such as Rahmatullah not only deny the authenticity of the passage of John 8:1–11, they also claim that the gospel according to John together with all his other writings were rejected by 'Allogin,[18] a sect of Christians in the second century.'[19]

Here is the argument in summary. First, some manuscripts do not contain particular short passages; therefore the Bible is corrupted. Second, that a particular group, regarded as heretical by all other Christians, denied the integrity of John's narrative, is considered strong evidence that the Bible is corrupted. If this type of reasoning by some Muslims is accepted, then it establishes a precedent.

If the notion of one obscure sect disowning John's gospel is a proof of the corruption of the Bible, then a similar accusation can also be levelled against the Qur'an. The *Memoniah* sect in the early days of Islam did not accept

---

[18] A learned presbyter by the name of Gaius, and those who agreed with him in his point of view, were called *Alogi* (F. F. Bruce, *The Canon of the Scriptures*, pp.169, 175, 178).

[19] Rahmatullah, *Izharul Haqq*, p.45.

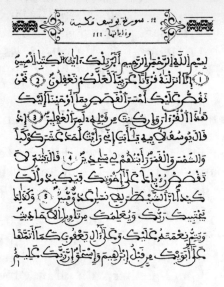

Figure 13. Surah Yusuf

The first few verses of Surah Yusuf which contains 111 verses. The Memoniah did not accept this surah as part of the Qur'an.

Surah Yusuf as part of the Qur'anic Scripture[20] (Chapter 12 in the present Qur'an).

In the records of Muslim writers, there are many indications that the present Qur'an is incomplete. Many verses and several whole chapters which were included in some copies of the Qur'an, yet are not available in the present official Qur'an. For example, consider Ubayy ibn Ka'b (about whom the *Sahih* of Al-Bukhari states that of all Muslims he was acknowledged to be one of the best Qur'anic reciters[21]). We find that his copy of the Qur'an contained a vast number of verses that were different from

---

[20] Imam Abu Zahrah, *Islami Madhahib* (Urdu tr.), p.133.
[21] *Sahih al-Bukhari*, Vol. 6, p.489.

Figure 14. The first and the last two chapters of the Qur'an
Ibn Masood did not treat these chapters as part of the Qur'an.

the official text of Uthman, but which often agreed with
Ibn Masood's text. Ibn Masood's Qur'an, as mentioned
above, did not include the first and the last two Surahs of
the present Qur'an (see illustration 14). On the other hand
Ubayy's copy included two extra Surahs namely *Al-Hafd*,
the Haste and *Al-Khal*, the Separation. A version of *Al-
Khal*, though not part of the present Qur'an, is still recited
in the late evening prayer of the day, *Isha*.[22]

According to Abdal Malik b. Marwan, Ali Ibn Abi Talib
included a Surah known as *al-Khafdh* in his copy of the
Qur'an. However, no such Surah is part of the present
Qur'an.

Abu Musa Ash'ari, who was one of the early authorities

22 Suyuti, *Al-Itqan fii Ulum al-Qur'an*, Vol.1, p.153,186.

(سورة الحفد)

أللَّهُمَّ إِيَّاكَ نَعْبُدُ ٥ وَلَكَ نُصَلِّي وَ نَسْجُدْ ٥ وَإِلَيْكَ نسْعَى وَ نَحْفِدُ ٥

نَرْجُو رَحْمَتَكَ ٥ وَ نَخْشَى عَذَابَكَ ٥ إِنَّ عَذَابَكَ بِالْكُفَّارِ مُلْحَقٌ ٥

(سوره الخلع)

أللَّهُمَّ إِنَا نَسْتَعِينُكَ وَ نَسْتَغْفِرُكَ ٥ وَنُثْنِي عَلَيْكَ ولَا نَكْفُرُكَ ٥

نَخْلَعُ وَ نَتْرُكُ مَنْ يَفْجُرُكَ ٥

Figure 15. A version of Surah al-Hafd and al-Khal

A version of Surah al-Hafd and al-Khal. Although they are not part of the present Qur'an, they are still recited in the late evening prayer of the day. It is believed that they appeared in the copies of the Qur'an of Ibn Kab and Ibn Abbas

on the Qur'an, is reported as saying, 'We used to recite a Surah which resembled in length and severity to *Bara'at . . .* I remember out of it: "If there were two valleys full of riches, for the son of Adam, he would long for a third valley, and nothing would fill the stomach of the son of Adam but dust."[23] *Bara'at* (Surah 9), also known as *Tauba*, has one hundred and twenty-nine verses. In other words, a whole Surah of similar length was revealed to Muhammad and recited by earlier Muslims but is not included in the present Qur'an.

---

[23] *Sahih al-Muslim*, Vol. 2, p.501.

Ibn Abi Hatim related an account he had heard from Abu Musa Ash'ari, 'We were reading a Surah which we used to liken to one of the rosaries, so we did not forget it. I memorised parts of it; "O you who believe! Say not what you do not do, for it will be written as a witness in your necks; you will be held accountable, and so you will be asked about it on the day of Judgement." '[24]

There are seventy three verses in *Ahzab* (Surah 73) today and yet it used to be equal in length to Baqarah (Surah 2) which has two hundred and eighty six verses.[25] Some of the Shia sect of Islam accuse Uthman and his commission of corrupting the Qur'an and expunging many important passages from it. In their writings, they claim that two whole chapters, *Wilayah* and *Nurain*, along with several whole and incomplete verses, have been omitted from the Qur'an. One wonders if this incompleteness is the reason why Abdullah Ibn Umar (d.693) said, 'Let no man say,' "I have learned the whole of the Qur'an!" How can he have learned the whole of it when much of it has been lost? Let him say, "I have learned what is extant of it".[26]

So we see that while most of the compilers omitted or lost some of the Qur'an, a few others did not. All this shows how easily a criticism which is used to condemn the Bible can also be used against the Qur'an. If, after all this, the Qur'an can still be called authentic and 'word for word' the word of God – as the majority of Muslims still believe – then a reconsideration of opinion about the Bible is also needed from these same Muslims.

---

[24] Suyuti, *Al-Itqan fi Ulum al-Qur'an*, Vol. 2, pp.52–69.

[25] Suyuti, *Al-Itqan fi Ulum al-Qur'an*, Vol. 1, p.524.

[26] Suyuti, *Al-Itqan fi Ulum al-Qur'an*, Vol.1, p.524.

Lost portions of the Bible

Many Muslim scholars claim that some writings that were once parts of the Scriptures have now been lost, and this is a proof of its incompleteness. They refer to those parts of the Old Testament section of the Bible where the names of some books are mentioned. For example, *The Book of Wars* (Numbers 21:14), *The Book of Jasher* (Joshua 10:13), *The History of Seer and Nathan* (1 Chronicles 29:29) and *Acts of Solomon* (1 Kings 11:14), etc.[27]

Christians do not have a proof nor seek to prove that these lost writings were part of the sacred Scriptures. The Jewish community never declared them to be part of their inspired Scriptures. However, if we follow the reasoning that these lost portions are a proof of the Bible being unreliable, then a similar question can be raised against the Qur'an. For example, Muhammad's wife, Aisha, said that among the revelations that were sent down, the verse of the ten breast feedings was abrogated by a verse which calls for five breast feedings. This verse was still read as part of the Qur'an at the time when the apostle of God died, meaning that the new revelation which abrogated the previous one was also lost.[28] How? Al-Hafiz Abi Abdullah Ibn Majah records that Aisha said that they (the lost verses) were under her bed. When Muhammad died and people became busy with the burial preparations, a domesticated animal entered and ate it.[29] This same story is mentioned by Dar-al-Qutni, al-Bazzar and al Tabarani, on the authority of Ibn Ishaq who heard it from Abdullah who himself heard it from Aisha.

---

[27] Rahmatullah, III, pp.165–169.

[28] *Sahih al-Muslim*, Vol. 2, p.740.

[29] *Sunnan Ibn Maja*, Vol. 1, Hadith 1944, p.626.

Suyuti writes, 'Hamida, the daughter of Abi Yunis said, "When my father was eighty years old, he read in the copy of Aisha, "God and his angel bless the prophet. O ye who believe, bless him and those who pray in the first rows." Then he said, "That was before Uthman changed the Qur'anic copies".'

In line with such reports, an extreme Shia group, the *Rafidis*, claimed that some 500 verses were lost from the Qur'an.[30] The number of verses in the present Qur'an are said to be 6247 (or 6360 if with each Surah the opening verse *Bismillah* is to be included).[31] However, al-Kulaini, the Shia *Muhadith*, who is recognised as being as great as Ismail al-Bukhari among the Sunni Muslims, relates in his work, *al-kafi fi'l-usul*, that the Qur'an which Gabriel brought to Muhammad contained seventeen thousand verses.[32]

So, if in spite of such reports the Qur'an can still be declared authentic then there should be no reason why the authenticity of the Christian Scriptures cannot also be accepted.

Contradiction within the text

Some Muslims reject the Bible as containing 'contradictory statements and teaching'. Such Muslims argue that if a book is to be treated as 'from God', (who would never countenance such diversity) then contradictory teaching is clear proof of the Bible's unworthiness.

Cited here are a few of these 'contradictions', together with a Christian response to each. Note that standard Muslim techniques, as applied to the Bible can also be used against contradictions within the text of the Qur'an.

---

[30] John Burton, *The collection of the Qur'an*, p.145.
[31] Qamar Naqvi, *Sahayef*, p.395.
[32] Manzoor Nomani, *Iranian Revolution*, p.169.

1. *The implication of all*

An apparent contradiction is found between Exodus 9:6 and 9:20,21. One verse implies that all the cattle of Egypt died, yet in the same chapter of the same book it is stated that some of the cattle did not perish.[33]

The context states that the plague was limited to animals 'in the field' (Exodus 9:3). Since many more cattle may have been in shelters or stables at the time, it can readily explain the existence of cattle among the Egyptians *after* the plague.

Muslims are somewhat disturbed by the term 'all' in this passage of the Bible. The term *all* is sometimes used in a loose sense to denote the majority or a great mass. In the Qur'an this convention is also used: 'And We showed Pharaoh all our signs, but he did reject and refuse.' (Surah 20:56). Surely God did not show him all the signs (*ayatena kullaaha*) which he is able to perform but he did perform those that were necessary. Similarly he killed enough of the cattle to make the point, but must have spared some.

2. *Mount Ararat*

'The water receded steadily from the earth. At the end of the hundred and fifty days the water had gone down, and on the seventeenth day of the seventh month the ark came to rest on the mountains of Ararat. The waters continued to recede until the tenth month, and on the first day of the tenth month the tops of the mountains became visible' (Genesis 8:3–5).

It is argued that this passage has 'a serious contradiction of facts, since the Ark could have not rested on the mountain in the seventh month . . . if the tops of the mountains could not be seen until the first day of the tenth month as described by the next verse.'[34]

---

[33] Rahmatullah, *Izharul Haqq*, part 2, p.6.

[34] Rahmatullah, *Izharul Haqq*, part 2, p.7.

Mount Ararat is situated in present day Turkey and is the highest mountain in that part of the world. It is possible that mount Ararat was still covered with water when the bottom of the ark ran aground upon it. One can assume that a considerable time would have elapsed for other mountain peaks to appear because of their lower elevation.

3. Satan or God?

In 2 Samuel 24:1 it is said that God moved David to number Israel, whereas in 1 Chronicles it is stated that it was Satan who provoked him to do so. Some Muslims in their conversation on this point pose a question, 'Is the Lord of David then Satan?'[35]

Anyone who has a reasonable knowledge of the Bible and the Qur'an can perceive that it is God who *allowed* Satan to provoke David into numbering Israel. When Satan provokes people, his action can also indirectly be described as the movement of God, for without his permission Satan would not be able to do these things. For instance, in the Book of Job it is mentioned that Satan was given power over Job to afflict him (Job 1:12) but God later speaks as if it was he himself who was moved against him (Job 2:3).

This should not be too difficult for Muslims as some of the last part of the Islamic creed known as *Al Imanul Mufassal* is: *Wal Qadri Khairihi wa Sharihi minal Lahi Ta'ala*, 'everything good and bad is decided by Allah'.[36] The Qur'an also says that God has given Satan permission until the day of Judgement to beguile people (Surah 38:79–85). Muslims believe that it is God who has appointed unto every prophet an adversary, devils of humankind and jinn, who inspire plausible discourse through guile (Surah 6:112; 22:51).

---

[35] Baagil, *Christian-Muslims Dialogue*, p.12.
[36] Ghulam Sarwar, *Islam: Beliefs and Teachings*, p.18.

4. In His image

Some Muslims find a contradiction between two passages in Genesis and Isaiah. The Bible states that God created human beings in his own image (Genesis 1:26), yet on the other hand the Bible contradicts it by suggesting that none is like him: 'To whom then will ye liken God? Or what likeness will ye compare unto him? . . . To whom then will ye liken me, or shall I be equal? saith the Holy One' (Isaiah 40:18, 25).[37]

However, the passage in Isaiah is a question aimed at those who worship idols made of wood and stone, while the passage in Genesis refers to the soul, that is, to the quality of human personality, the immaterial part. One conveys the idea of resemblance while the other is talking about equality. To suggest these passages are contradictory ignores these two completely different contexts.

5. Aaron died where?

Numbers 33:38 says that Aaron died at Mount Hor, however in Deuteronomy 10:6 it seems to suggest that Aaron died at Mosera. Bashir-ud-Din argues, 'It is evident that one and the same person could not die in two different places. There can be no doubt that these two contradictory passages were entered in the Bible by two different scribes who have written down their speculations in it and presented them as the Word of God.'[38]

Researchers believe that Mosera or Moseroth was a place near to Mount Hor, and within sight of it. During the encampment of the Israelites at Mosera, Aaron went up the hill and died. Mosera was also the general name of the district in which Mount Hor was situated.

---

[37] Baagil, *Christian-Muslim Dialogue*, p.13.

[38] Bashiruddin, *Introduction to the Study of the Holy Qur'an*, p.36.

6. God seen or not seen?

On the one hand the Bible states in many passages that people saw God; however it also tells us that He cannot be seen (Genesis 32:30; Exodus 24:9,10; Judges 13:22; Daniel 7:9 versus Exodus 33:20; Deuteronomy 4:15; John 1:13; 5:37; 1 Timothy 1:17; 6:16).

The Bible says that God is Spirit and thus invisible. His whole essence thus cannot be ascertained visually by the *outward* eye. However, he may let people see him in various ways as is mentioned in the passages where people said they saw God. Though they did not see God in his infinite essence, they perceived him in a restricted way, just as lightning is a visible and limited manifestation showing the existence of the invisible power of electricity. Since everything is possible for God, he can choose the form in which he wishes to partially reveal himself. For example, in the cases of Isaiah and Daniel, God chose that they should see him in visions. In some cases it was said merely that 'God was seen'; in others, some presence appears and is identified with God, as happened in certain places with Moses at Mount Sinai (Bible: Exodus 3:1–6; 24:15,16; Qur'an: Surah 20:9–48; 27:7–12; 28:29–35; 79:15–19).

7. Testimony valid or not?

Jesus said, 'If I testify about myself, my testimony is not valid' (John 5:31). In another place he said, 'Even if I testify on my own behalf, my testimony is valid . . .' (John 8:14).[39] How could Jesus say on the one hand that his lone testimony was not true and yet on the other that it was true?

Christians claim there is no discrepancy in the two statements. The context should be considered in order to determine what Jesus was actually saying. In both cases he is

---

[39] Baagil, *Christian-Muslim Dialogue*, p.13.

trying to make a persuasive case using the usual Mosaic requirement for at least two witnesses. The Mosaic Law required a minimum of two witnesses to constitute valid evidence (Deuteronomy 9:15; Matthew 18:16; John 8:17). He therefore admits that his own testimony alone would not be regarded as legal proof, then he proceeds to adduce the corroborative testimony of John the Baptist (John 5:34). He presents it, not because he is bound by a human rule about testimony, but because the hearers thought it necessary. Jesus' aim was that they might accept him and his message and so be saved. It is interesting to read in this context that though he has another witness, that is, God himself, he refers to John the Baptist's testimony. However in the later passage (John 8:14) he refers to the divine witness since he knows that his hearers have previously rejected the witness of John the Baptist (Matthew 21:25–28; Mark 11:30–33; Luke 20:3–7). While he does not need any human testimony to support his case (John 5:34), it is the people who need it. Thus it should not surprise us when he says to his disciples that the Holy Spirit 'will testify about me. And you also must testify, for you have been with me from the beginning' (John 15:26–27).

The Qur'anic contradictions

It is worth noting that the sort of contradictions found in the Bible can also be found in the Qur'an. Muslims will have answers to such Qur'anic contradictions just as Christians have answers to biblical contradictions. Only a few examples are sufficient to prove the point:

1. The Qur'an in several of its passages claim that it is in 'clear Arabic' so that people may understand (Surah 16:103). However, in another place it claims

that 'no one knows its explanation except Allah', *Wa ma yalamu tawilh ilal lah* (Surah 3:7).

2. In one passage Allah forbids Muslims to be kind to those who oppose them (Surah 58:22), yet they are commanded in another to be kind to them (Surah 31:15).

3. In some passages of the Qur'an it is stated that those who are Muslims, Jews, Christians and Sabaeans will have no fear and neither shall they grieve if they believe in God and the day of Judgement (Surah 2:69; 5:69); however, other passages tell us that Islam is the only religion acceptable to God (Surah 3:19; 5:85).

4. On the one hand the Qur'an says that there is no compulsion in religion (Surah 2:256; 10:99) yet on the other it has verses giving commands to fight others, Christians or Jews or idolaters, 'whoever ye find' (Surah 9:5,29).

5. In one passage Muslims are ordered not to take the Jews or Christians for friends (Surah 5:51), yet in the same context they are told that Christians are nearest to them in affection (Surah 5:82).

6. According to one passage no intercession will be accepted on the day of Judgement (Surah 2:48) and yet another passage suggests that it will be available (Surah 10:3).

7. In several passages Muhammad is mentioned as a warner to the Arabs to whom no warner came before him (Surah 28:48; 32:3; 36:6), but in other verses of the Qur'an we find that Allah did send warners to every nation (Surah 16:63).

8. On the day of Judgement, God will examine people of their deeds (Surah 37:24), however, another passage tells us that no question will be asked of man or Jinn as to his sin (Surah 55:40).

9. Humans have been created from dust, *turab*
   (Surah 35:12). Another passage suggests that
   human creation was from *sounding clay* and from
   mud moulded into shape (Surah 15:26). Elsewhere
   this clay is compared to pottery or sticky clay
   (Surah 55:13; 37:11).
10. Those who believe, in their hearts, they feel satis-
    faction in the remembrance of Allah (Surah 13:28),
    yet another passage teaches that when Allah is
    mentioned they feel a tremor of fear in their hearts
    (Surah 8:2).

The status of men of God

One reason why Muslims reject the Bible as the Word of
God is that it reports all the prophets (except Jesus) as
guilty of wrong doing. It attributes errors, adultery, forni-
cation and incest to holy men of God, like Adam, Noah,
Abraham, Lot, David, Solomon and many others. Muslims claim that the Qur'an does not mention any wrongdoing committed by these prophets but exalts these
people to the respect and honour they deserve.

Christians respond in the light of their own Scriptures,
saying that even a true prophet was only free of blasphemy and lying when communicating the messages of
God. Christians do not deny that these men of God were
subject to errors, negligence, and forgetfulness in their
ordinary daily affairs. Yet they insist, nevertheless, that
the prophets *were* inspired.

Most of the people who are mentioned in the Bible as
having committed sin are also recorded as having become
sorry and repented of what they had done. The Bible does
not say that all people of God did wrong. For example,
Enoch, Elijah, Joseph, Daniel and many others are

mentioned without any sin being attributed to them in the Bible. However, silence is not a proof of the absence of sin. Jesus is positively described as without sin.

The Qur'an also attributes sin to some of the prophets but not in such detail as is included in the Bible. This is hardly evidence that these people were *masoom*, innocent. The Qur'an says that the wife of Potiphar passionately desired him and likewise Joseph too, *Wa laqad ham'mat bihi wa ham'ma biha* (Surah 12:23–35). However, the Bible tells us that Joseph refused her advances, 'How can I do this great wickedness and sin against God?' (Genesis 39:9).

The Bible should not be discredited just because it uncovers, along with the many good deeds done by people, many of their bad deeds as well. The reason for showing both sides of the story is that complete holiness is only attributable to God. Only God has provided a way of dealing with sin. The popular tradition that prophets and godly men are *masoom*, innocent, in fact contradicts the Qur'an. Sin is after all sin, whether small or big. The Qur'an reports several men of God asking for mercy and forgiveness from God for their sin and wrongdoing which they freely admit:

1. Adam: Surah 2:37; 7:22–23
2. Noah: Surah 71:24–28; 11:47–49
3. Moses: Surah 7:146–150; 20:40, 87–95; 28:16
4. Solomon: Surah 38:30–34
5. David: Surah 38:20–32
6. Jonah: Surah 37:142; 21:87–88
7. Abraham: Surah 6:77–78; 26:82; 37:86–89
8. Muhammad: Surah 47:19; 48:1–2

According to the Qur'an all these saintly people committed wrongdoing and asked God for forgiveness. If they had not committed anything wrong, then the question of forgiveness would not arise. In at least two passages, the

Qur'an states that Satan tempted ordinary believers and prophets as well (Surah 32:36; 22:52), although temptation need not have actually led to wrongdoing. Therefore, the Bible cannot be rejected just because it goes into the detail of why some men of God asked him for forgiveness and remission of their wrong doings.

Some Muslims are upset that Noah has been reported in the Bible as drinking wine, but how easily they forget that even Muslims drank wine at the beginning of Islam. So much so that they performed prayers when intoxicated, not knowing what they were doing and Muhammad had to forbid them through a Qur'anic revelation (Surah 4:43). Similarly Muslims have difficulty with Lot's incestuous activities as recorded in Genesis 19:30–38. It could be argued, however, that the guilty party was not Lot but his daughters. However, the Qur'an also shows Lot in a bad light, offering his daughters to adulterers and fornicators of his tribe to save his guests. It is difficult, however, to adjudicate on the social habits of those days.

The incident of Lot is mentioned in two places in the Qur'an. In one passage (Surah 11:78) it says, 'And his people came rushing towards him, and they had been long in the habit of practising abominations. He said, "O my people! Here are my daughters: they are purer for you (if ye marry)." ' However, in another passage (Surah 15:71) the Qur'an states that Lot said to them, 'There are my daughters (to marry), if ye must act (so).'

To reduce the sense of embarrassment, the translator, Yusuf Ali, has added the words in brackets which are not actually in the text of the Qur'an at all. This 'amendment' is a far more blatant amendment of the text than the accusations levelled at Christians by Muslims, when they see perceived differences between translations. Other commentators say that what Lot meant was that they should marry his daughters, but how could they marry all the people of the tribe? Above all, those wicked people had come with the intent of committing abominations with his guests and in such a situation to offer his daughters for 'marriage' is a somewhat far-fetched idea. However, the duty of protecting guests is well understood.

Incompatible narratives

Many Muslims in their quest to reject the Bible refer to narratives which show 'incompatibility'. They ignore the fact that sometimes the narrative may not be exact, but the nub of the matter, or its message, is the same. For example, the case of the blind men at Jericho in the Christian Scriptures; the Gospel according to Matthew relates how two blind men met Jesus, while both Mark and Luke mention only the one who had faith. The detail may seem contradictory but neither of these statements denies the other. The Qur'anic example of a similar case is of Adam and Eve's expulsion. In one passage it is stated that God said to them, 'Get ye down all (*Uhbitu*) from here', yet in another passage God is mentioned to have said, 'Get ye down both (*Uhbita*) of you' (Surah 2:38; 20:123). In both cases the figures and narratives are not identical but the heart of the matter is the same. Let us now consider some of the objections and responses to these so-called incompatibilities.

1. *The two accounts of Jesus' birth*
In line with some western critics Muslim writers say that the two accounts of Jesus' birth (Matthew 2 and Luke 2) are incompatible, since Matthew omits the residence at Nazareth before the nativity, the circumstances which brought Joseph and Mary to Bethlehem and the presentation in the temple; while Luke does not mention the visit of the Magi, the murder of the innocents, nor the flight to

Egypt. Thus they conclude that neither of the two narratives are reliable and therefore neither can be inspired.[40]

Just because the narrative according to Luke does not mention the journey to Egypt or other information does not mean that it did not take place. If the two had agreed on every detail, sceptics would then have accused the two writers of having conspired. The variation found between Matthew and Luke points to their integrity. Christians believe that both accounts are free from error. All that happened is that neither narrative includes every detail that took place. After reading Matthew 2 and Luke 2, the probable order of events were as follows:

1. The annunciation during residence at Nazareth
2. Journey of Joseph and Mary from Nazareth to Bethlehem
3. Birth of Jesus
4. Presentation at the temple in Jerusalem
5. Visit of Magi
6. Flight to Egypt
7. Return and settlement at Nazareth

If differences between a detailed and a summarised narrative of the same event (or events) are said to point to the unreliability of the Bible, then similar cases can be found in the Qur'an as well. For instance, the story of Moses is given in at least eight places in the Qur'an in varying detail. Let us take Surah 20 and Surah 79. While the first is quite detailed, the latter omits several salient points.

Moses and the fire in a bush; the gift of miracles; Aaron's dedication as assistant; recalling the favours; the sending of both Aaron and Moses to Pharaoh; the display of miracles; Pharaoh's disobedience and God's punishment. (Surah 20: 9 ff)

[40] Rahmatullah, *Izharul Haqq*, part 2, p.24.

The Story of Moses: The call of Moses (no mention of the fire in the bush, of Aaron and miracles; no mention of past favours); Moses being sent to Pharaoh (Aaron not mentioned); the sign shown by Moses (no detail); Pharaoh's disobedience and God's punishment (no detail). (Surah 79: 15ff)

One narrative has many details while the other narrative just presents the gist of the whole story. If, in spite of such omissions and additions of material and difference in the two narratives, the Qur'an can be taken to be reliable and inspired, then Muslims can hardly dispute the veracity of the Christian Scriptures on such grounds.

2. *The plea of the Roman officer*
One Bible passage says that when Jesus came into Capernaum, an army officer came asking him to heal his servant (Matthew 8:5). However, another passage reads that he sent some elders of the Jews to him (Luke 7:3).[41] Did the army officer speak to Jesus, or did he send somebody else to speak to him? Muslims argue that the two reports of the same occasion are incompatible.

The army officer perhaps delivered his message to Jesus through the elders of the Jews. It is also possible that he himself came after he had sent the elders to Jesus. Matthew mentioned the army officer because he was the one in need. Luke mentions the Jews because they were the first to come to Jesus. Why does one passage say that the man himself entreated Jesus? Because the elders served as his mouthpiece.

These two passages may simply reflect cultural differences in narration style: Matthew was a Jew while Luke is thought by many to have been Greek. It is usually understood that the deed which a person tells others to do is in

---

[41] Rahmatullah, *Izharul Haqq*, part 2, p.58.

effect done by him. For example, what a leader of a group, a community or a country does is in reality done by those he delegates. An Old Testament passage may be found in 2 Chronicles 3:1 where it is stated that Solomon started to build the house of God in Jerusalem. Later, it is said, 'Solomon . . . finished the temple of the Lord' (2 Chronicles 7:11). Now Solomon personally did not build the temple from start to finish. The actual building work was done by a multitude of craftsmen and labourers. However, Solomon as the organiser was the one responsible. Hence the Bible says that he built the house. In the same way the passage in Matthew tells us that the military officer approached Jesus but the passage in Luke gives the added detail that he approached Jesus *through* the Jewish elders. There is another example of Jesus' disciples baptising, yet it was said that Jesus baptised (John 4:1–2).

3. Cain and his family
The Bible states that Adam and Eve had two sons, Cain and Abel. Cain killed Abel. If Adam and Eve had only two sons, where did Cain find his wife (Genesis 4:1,2; 4:17)?

The answer lies in the fact that Adam and Eve had more than two children. They had a large family. In Genesis 5:3 it is said that Adam became father to another son named Seth and then in the following verse that he became father to sons and daughters (Genesis 5:4). So Cain could have married one of his own sisters or even one of his nieces. If such an explanation is not accepted then one may ask: has the Qur'an any better idea of the origin of these wives?

4. Faith and works
Ephesians 2:8–9 states that Christians are saved by grace not by works: 'For it is by grace that you have been saved, through faith . . . not by works'. However another passage insists on the importance of works: 'As the body without

the spirit is dead, so faith without deeds is dead' (James 2:26). How can Christians reconcile these two statements?[42]

The context of both passages shows that one statement complements the other. One is referring to the efforts of the Jews to keep the Mosaic Law. They believed that if they kept the Law in all its details, then they would be righteous. However, the text shows that people can never become righteous through their own efforts alone. They can only be saved by faith in Jesus. The later passage adds the vital point that faith itself is of no value if not supported by actions. One who has faith in Jesus should prove it by what he does. An inactive faith is a dead faith and will not lead to salvation.

5. *The torture stake*

It is claimed that there is a contradiction between Luke's and John's narratives. In John's Gospel, it is said of Jesus: 'Carrying his own cross, he went out' (John 19:17). However, Luke says: 'As they led him away, they seized Simon of Cyrene, who was on his way in from the country, and put the cross on him and made him carry it behind Jesus' (Luke 23:26). Did Jesus carry the implement of his death, or did Simon carry it for him?[43]

To begin with, Jesus evidently carried his own cross, as John points out. As he made his way through the streets of Jerusalem, he collapsed from exhaustion, owing to his previous scourging. It was then, as Matthew, Mark and Luke testify, that Simon of Cyrene carried the cross for him.

---

[42] Arfaque Malik, A Beam in their Eyes, *The Straight Path*, June 1988, Birmingham.

[43] Bilal Philips, *The True Message of Jesus Christ*, pp.27–28 (Dar al-Fatah, 1996).

6. Genealogy of Jesus Christ

Some Muslims claim that there is a contradiction between the genealogies of Jesus in Matthew and Luke because there is a vast difference in the names the two narrators have listed.[44] Deedat, for instance, says that such a difference obviously proves them 'confounded liars.'[45]

Matthew (who was writing for a Jewish audience) records the genealogy of Jesus through Joseph's line. He concentrates on Joseph's role as his natural guardian. Joseph was not his actual father but he had to be regarded as his father as most Jews reckoned their genealogies through their fathers. Luke (who was writing for a non-Jewish audience) concentrates on the genealogy of Jesus through Mary, as mentioned in Luke 3:23. Throughout the list of ancestors he names, there is no mention of a woman. Though he concentrates on Mary's role in the birth of Jesus, he does not describe Jesus as the son of Mary but as the 'supposed son of Joseph'. In Luke's narrative the word *supposed* indicates that it was not the actual genealogy of Joseph that was being recorded.

Objections against the style and expression

Some Muslims argue that since the style and expressions of the writers of the different parts of the Bible are not identical, the Bible as a whole cannot be treated as the word of God. They claim that this variation in itself is evidence of corruption, error and inconsistency in the Bible.[46] Christians assert that if such a uniformity had occurred during its production, the accusers would have then argued that the style and expression suggests that it

---

[44] Bilal Philips, p.30.
[45] Deedat, *Is the Bible God's Word?*, p.54.
[46] Rahmatullah, *Izharul Haqq*, part 3, p.11.

was written by one person and at one time. It is inconceivable that God's inspiration should be limited to one style.

Christians further claim that although the people who wrote the Bible came from different times, various and distant places, yet there is unity in their message, a unity of purpose and harmony of faith. They differ in their style and eloquence but their teaching and purpose remained one. All of them referred to salvation and the re-establishment of peoples' relationship and fellowship with God. These people, Christians claim, spoke/wrote as they were moved to by the Holy Spirit (2 Peter 1:21).

The Bible is different from other books in its unity. That unity is not expressed in terms of its style and expression but in its overall message. Christians see it from beginning to end as one unfolding story of God's plan of salvation for people through Jesus (John 14:6). To them, the Old Testament is the preparation (John 5:39,46,47; Luke 24:44; Isaiah 40:3) and the Gospels are the manifestation of this plan (John 1:29). The early propagation of this message is recorded in the Acts of the Apostles (Acts 1:8). The Epistles give explanations (Colossians 1:27) and lastly the book of Revelation is a vision of the consummation (Revelation 1:7). The Bible, Christians believe, therefore reveals the nature of God in his acts in creation, history, and in the person of Jesus.

Considering the style of the text in the Bible, some argue that God and the recipients of revelations are mentioned in the third person in the books of the Bible. Some Muslims argue that the use of the first person would certainly have made the books more respectable and trustworthy. To them 'a statement made in the first person by the author carries more weight and value than his statement made by someone else in the third person.'[47]

---

[47] Rahmatullah, *Izharul Haqq*, part 1, pp.23–24.

Such an argument would militate equally against the integrity of the Qur'an. To Muslims, God is the author of the Qur'an and yet in it his speech is reported in the third person in many passages. Every chapter of the Qur'an but one begins with the praise of God in the third person. The whole first chapter and several of the chapters towards the end of the Qur'an mention God *in the third person*. Even in the middle Surahs, God frequently refers to himself as 'He', 'Allah', 'the merciful' and so on. Would these critics then accept that such parts of the Qur'an are less reliable? If this test does not invalidate the Qur'an, it cannot invalidate the Bible either.

The human elements and errors in Scriptures

Muslims believe that because a revelation is the word of God there is nothing human in it. The popular assumption is that the Qur'an is made up of words cited verbatim from God while the Bible contains some words from God but mostly from mere people. Some Muslims do accept that recorded instances in the Bible of the direct speech of God and of the prophets does represent an element of inspiration.

The modern conservative Maulana Mawdudi states that no corruption is possible wherever direct speech is reported in the Bible.[48] This would mean that only those passages recorded verbatim are the inspired words of God while other statements are the words of narrators or other people, and thus cannot be trusted as inspired. However, such a view also works against the Qur'an. The very first verse, *Bismillah* (in the name of Allah), suggests somebody other than God himself is speaking. Like the Bible, the

---

[48] Mawdudi, *Tafhim al-Qur'an*, Vol. 1, pp.231–232, (Lahore: Idara Islamiat, 1973).

Qur'an has words and dialogues involving other people, the words of angels, the words of prophets and even words of the disciples of Christ. It has the words of the Jews, of Christians, from the unbelievers of Makkah and even of Muhammad.

The Qur'an also contains the words of the companions of Muhammad treated as the verbatim words of God. From the traditions and the history of ear ly Islam, we learn that Umar ibn al-Khattab played a major role in the revelation of the Qur'an. Many times Umar would make a suggestion or say something to Muhammad and a revelation would come. Sometimes, the revelation was revealed using the same words and vocabulary of Umar. He himself admitted it to friends, saying for example, that when the verses *Wa Laqad Khalaqna al insan* (Man We did create from a quintessence of clay) was revealed, he exclaimed, *Fatabarakallhu ahsanul khaliqin,* (So blessed be Allah, the best to create!) and God revealed the same urah 23:12,14).[49]

At times Muhammad was even willing to reverse God's command to accommodate Umar's suggestions. For instance, *Sahih Muslim* relates the tradition that once Muhammad sent Abu Huraira to tell people the good news that all who testify that there is no god but Allah, being assured of it in their hearts, shall go to paradise. The first person Abu Huraira met was Umar and told him what the Prophet had said. Umar was enraged and struck him on the chest and ordered him to go back to the Prophet. Huraira went back to the Prophet and complained. The Prophet asked Umar for the reason for striking Huraira. Instead of replying, Umar asked the Prophet, 'Did you send Abu Huraira to tell people who testified that there is no god but Allah, and being assured of it in their heart, the tidings that they would surely go to

---

[49] Suyuti, *Al-Itqan fi Ulum al-Qur'an,* Vol. 1, p.89.

paradise?' He said, 'Yes'. Umar pleaded with the Prophet: 'Please don't do it, for I am afraid that people will trust in it alone; let them go on doing good deeds.' Muhammad agreed and said, 'Well, let them.'[50] One wonders what other revelation the Prophet cancelled at the request of his companions.

Many times the revelation came according to what Muhammad would himself wish and desire. This situation was acutely felt by his companions, so much so that when Surah 33:51 was revealed, his wife, Aisha, complained to him, 'I feel that your Lord hastens in fulfilling your wishes and desires.'[51]

Some Muslims quote Christian and non-Christian writers, saying that the Bible has copyist errors. They claim that such errors are a proof of why they should not trust the integrity of the Bible. For example, it is argued that on the one hand it says that Michal, the daughter of Saul, had no children (2 Samuel 6:23) but another passage states that she had five sons (2 Samuel 21:8). How could it be that at one place the Bible describes her as childless and yet she is the mother of five sons in another passage?[52]

Michal reviled God and David. In punishment she bore no *more* children from there on. One opinion is that the five sons mentioned in the latter passage were brought up by Michal but were the children of her sister, Merab, the wife of Adriel (1 Samuel 18:19). However, most commentators believe that the later passage does not refer to Michal at all but rather to Merab, Saul's other daughter. It is a copyist's error in the Hebrew text. Christians willingly admit that the Bible contains copyists' errors, but they add that it does not interfere with the heart of the message of their Scripture.

---

[50] *Sahih al-Muslim*, Vol 1, p.24
[51] *Sahih al-Bukhari*, Vol. 6, p.295.
[52] Baagil, *Christian-Muslim Dialogue*, p.12.

It can be argued that if copyists' errors can be taken as evidence to discredit the Bible, then the same can be said of all Scriptures which claim to be inspired. The Qur'an also contains copyists' errors. For example, Arabists know that the word *muqimin* (performers) in Surah 4 verse 162 is the odd word out. It has been used in the objective rather than the subjective form. Even Muhammad's wife, Aisha, said that it was a copyist's error.[53] She also added that Muhammad used to recite the word *mutoon* (alms) in this verse as *yatoona ma'to* (those who bring whatever they received).[54]

Ibn Abbas used to recite the word *yatabayaneladhina* (has become distinct) instead of *yayaseladhina* (have come to know) in Surah 13:31. When people enquired, he insisted on his recitation and declared that the Qur'anic reading was a copyist's error, saying, 'I think when the copyist wrote this verse, he was sleepy.'[55] Suyuti in his *Itqan* gives a long list of variant readings and copyists' errors in the Qur'an.[56]

It can be demonstrated that even the Uthmanic recension of the Qur'an contains copyists' errors. By comparison between the available information on the earlier texts of the Qur'an and the present text, it can be shown that the differences actually change the meaning of words and phrases. However, if this does not affect the integrity of the Qur'an, then neither does it affect the Bible.

Contradictions between versions

To prove that alteration and corruption has occurred during the production of the present Bible, some Muslims

[53] Suyuti, *Al-Itqan fi Ulum al-Qur'an*, Vol. 1, p.492.
[54] Suyuti, *Al-Itqan fi Ulum al-Qur'an*, Vol. 1, p.497.
[55] Suyuti, *Al-Itqan fi Ulum al-Qur'an*, Vol. 1, p.498.
[56] Suyuti, *Al-Itqan fi Ulum al-Qur'an*, Vol. 1, p.490–500.

direct their argument to different versions of the Bible available in the English language. For example, in his book, *Is the Bible God's Word?*, Deedat's main source of material to discredit the Bible, is his comparison between two English translations. To prove that the Bible is corrupt, he and several others quote statements from the preface of the Revised Standard Version to prove that the King James version of the Bible has defects[57] and 'so many and so serious as to call for revision of the English translation.'[58] Similarly, many in their discussions argue that since one version is accepted more widely than the other, this is evidence that there is something wrong with the Bible.

A Christian response is that 'version' here is another way of saying 'translation'. These versions are only translations. The Qur'an is also available in several English 'translations' and from time to time these translations are edited and improved; for example Yusaf Ali's translation, Moulvi Muhammad Ali's translation, Moulvi Sher Ali's translation, Muhammad Asad's translation of the Qur'an and many more are readily available. Like many Christian groups, one translation is accepted by one group of Muslims yet is rejected by others. Though Muhammad Ali's translation has been proscribed and confiscated by the ministry of religious affairs in Pakistan, there are still people who prefer it. Similarly, in 1978, when Asad's translation was introduced in South Africa, some of the Muslim leaders vehemently opposed it. Yet many copies were sold and this translation is still in print. The translation of the Qur'an into Urdu by Moulvi Raza Ahmad Khan (with a commentary by Moulana Naeemuddin) is another example: it was banned in Saudi Arabia and among certain

---

[57] Deedat, *Is the Bible God's Word?*, p.11.
[58] Bilal Philips, *The True Message of Jesus Christ*, p.12.

circles in Pakistan. In spite of all this, no one claims that the Qur'an was corrupted. It should be realised that from time to time both Muslims and Christians become aware of the need to extend or revise their translations.

Corruption in translation

One of the more serious objections is that different versions of the Bible give different meanings to the Greek and Hebrew texts. One translation may appear to differ totally from another. The best example of this to many Muslims is John 3:16. The King James Version has the expression 'only begotten Son' whereas the Revised Standard Version mentions 'only Son' and has removed the word 'begotten'. Thus it is believed by some Muslims to be a corruption or alteration. Others take the removal of the word 'begotten' as such an improvement that it brings the Bible 'a degree nearer to the Qur'anic truth.'[59]

This is a matter of translation. The Greek word can mean 'unique Son'; there is no difference in the original Greek, and little difference in the two translations in presenting the nearest understanding. Muslims believe that the Qur'an denies that Jesus is the son of God but there is little point in claiming that the Revised Standard Version has come nearer to the Qur'anic teaching.

Such a change in translation can also be seen for the text of the Qur'an. Yusuf Ali, for example, translates Surah Mariam 19:88 as 'God Most Gracious has begotten a Son', but Muhammad Marmaduke Pickthal, Moulvi Muhammad Ali, Moulvi Daryabadi, Moulvi Malik Farid and Muhammad Asad have chosen the word *taken* instead of *begotten*. Thus there are two different translations of an

---

[59] Deedat, *Is the Bible God's Word?*, p.16.

Arabic word of the Qur'an. This choice of word in translation does not mean that the Qur'an is corrupted, and so
the same can be said of the Bible.

Another example is of Surah 5:44. Muhammad
Marmaduke Pickthal's translation is: 'Lo! We did reveal
the Torah, where *is* guidance and light', however, Yusuf
Ali translates the same verse in the past tense saying, 'It
was We who revealed the Law (to Moses): therein *was*
guidance and light.' (Surah 5:47). Yusuf Ali translates
another verse of the Qur'an like this: 'We sent him (Jesus)
the Gospel, therein *was* guidance and light' (Surah 5:49).
The same is translated by Pickthal as 'We bestowed on him
the Gospel wherein *is* guidance and a light.'

In one passage (Surah 4:4) the words *Huddal-linnaas* are
used for the Torah and Injil and are translated by Yusuf Ali
as 'as a guide to mankind' implying within its context that
validity applies only in the past. Note, however, that the
same two words when used for the Qur'an (Surah 2:185)
are made to include the present and future tense as well.

In another place, the words *Wa Hudan wa Maw'izatal-lil-
muttaqin* (a guidance and admonition to those who fear
God) are used for the Torah (Surah 5:49) and elsewhere the
very same words appear to describe the Qur'an (Surah
3:138). However, for the Torah the English interpretation
is in the *past tense* while in the case of the Qur'an it is in the
present tense. These examples are given just to show how
easily a test which is used against one set of Scriptures can
be used against another.

Conclusion

After looking at the questions of errors, contradictions,
variant readings and textual historicity of the Scriptures,
one can comfortably come to the conclusion that the

process of compilation of the Qur'an and the Bible was similar. If the Bible is rejected by Muslims because of certain reservations, then these same reservations can similarly be applied to the Qur'an to discredit it. As there are people who claim that parts of the Bible are lost, there are those like Muhammad's companions, as well as the rightly guided caliphs and many other prominent Muslim scholars of Islam who acknowledge that parts of the Qur'an were lost. If one is to reject the Bible on suspicion of its being subjected to alteration, then the same can be said about the Qur'an. If the Bible is rejected just because some people or sects have rejected parts of it, then the same can be said of Muhammad's companions; and, later, their companions who also disagreed over chapters, verses and phrases within the Qur'an. If, in spite of such a situation, Muslims can claim that the Qur'an's message is intact, then they must surely concede that it is also possible that the essential message of the Bible is also entire and impeccably preserved.

6

Are these truly the Scriptures?

When Christians use the testimony of the Qur'an in support of the Bible's integrity, some Muslims argue that the references in the Qur'an do not relate to present day versions of the Torah and the Gospel. They say that the 'Scriptures' which Christians and Jews had at the time of Muhammad (571–632 CE), were different from those available today. In effect, they are saying that the Jews of Muhammad's day were reading a different Torah, something which was 'certainly not identical', 'nor resembled anything like the Old Testament' which contains the reports, stories and myths of groups of people gone by. Similarly the Injil (Gospel) was 'not at all identical with the New Testament or even the four gospels' available to us today[1] which have pagan origins.[2]

It is stated that when the Qur'an talks about a single book known as the Gospel (as given to Jesus) and a single book as given to Moses (known as the Torah) that they were not the four gospels as we find them in the New Testament nor the first five books of the Old Testament known today as the Torah. To conclude the matter, such Muslims add that even the title 'Bible' for the Scriptures of

---

[1] Izzat Khan and Abu Abdullah, *Divine Revelations, The Muslims and the Bibles: A Clarification*, pp.4–6.
[2] Kamal-ud-Din, *The Sources of Christianity*, p.15.

the Jews and Christians is foreign to the Qur'an and it is not *that Scripture* which is mentioned in the Qur'an as containing guidance and light. We will now consider some of the points of such argument and then give a Christian response to them.

Is the Bible unknown to the Qur'an?

Can we accept statements like, 'The Qur'anic passages which testify to the Torah, the Injil and the Psalms, do not refer to what Christians now call the Bible?' It is indeed true that the title 'Bible' is not used in the Qur'an although it has used its own transliteration of the title 'Bible'. Any good dictionary will explain that the word *Bible* is derived from the Greek word *biblia* (neuter plural), which means 'books'. As the collections of Jewish and Christian texts came increasingly to be considered as one unit, the term in Latin began to be understood as feminine singular, denoting 'The Book'. The same word has come through to modern English in words like bibliography. So when the title *Bible*, the book, was used, it denoted a collection of writings or books of the Christian and Jewish Scriptures.

The phrase *'al-Kitab'* is translated as *the book*. The Qur'an does not contain the proper title, 'Bible' for the Scriptures of the Jews and Christians but has identified it as *'Kitab'* (the Book) by calling the followers as *'Ahlal Kitab'*, the people of the Book. The Qur'an has borrowed many foreign terms and names like *Tawrat, Furqan, Injil, Isa* and *Musa* etc.; and Arabized them into its text. When it came to using the word *Bible*, however, it contains its own Arabic words derived from Hebrew and Aramaic, thus calling the Jews and Christians *'Ahlal Kitab'*, the people of the Book, and referring to their Scripture not only as 'the Book', *Kitab*, but also listing the parts of it as the *Tawrah*,

Zaboor, Injil and *Sahaif* (Torah, Psalms, the Gospel(s) and the books of the prophets respectively).

Therefore the notion that the Qur'an does not mention the Bible is simply wrong. It will be like saying that the Qur'an does not mention 'God'. The Muslim listener will refer to many verses where Arabic words like '*Allah*' or '*Rab*' are mentioned. If those words stand for God in the Qur'an then it should not be difficult to recognise that the words *Ahlal Kitab* stands for Jews and Christians and their *Kitab* stands for their Scriptures – the Bible – in the contexts as referred to them in the Qur'an.

The single Injil and Torah

Muslim writers contend that the original Pentateuch and the original Gospel have disappeared and became extinct from the world. This claim is expanded by asserting, 'We strictly deny that the original Torah (Pentateuch) and the original Evangel existed at the time of the Prophet Muhammad and that they were not changed until later.'[3] Such people say further, 'The present gospels, chronicles and epistles are certainly not the Evangel referred to by the Holy Qur'an and so they are not, as such, acceptable to the Muslims.'[4]

The Muslim commentator, Yusuf Ali, claims that 'the *Injil* (Greek, *Evangel* = Gospel) spoken of by the Qur'an is not the New Testament. It is not the four Gospels now received as canonical. It is the single Gospel which, Islam teaches, was revealed to Jesus, and which he taught. Fragments of it survive in the received canonical Gospels . . .'[5]

---

[3] Rahmatullah, *Izharul Haqq*, Part III, p.30.

[4] Rahmatullah, *Izharul Haqq*, Part III, p.31.

[5] Yusuf Ali, *The Holy Qur'an: English Translation of the Meaning and Commentary*, p.334).

Christians believe there is indeed one *Injil*, brought by Jesus, the Christ. The word *Injil* in Arabic is a transliteration of the Greek *Evangelion* as Yusuf Ali has rightly mentioned in his statement. The Greek word *Evangelion* means 'happy message' or 'good news'. Distinguished Muslim commentators like Baidhawi and Zamakhshari openly admit that *Injil* is not an Arabic word but is derived from the Syriac and/or the Greek word Evangel – the Gospel, the good news. Taking this as true, one should look no further than among those who have been using this term for their Scriptures in Muhammad's time and even before then. Looking at such evidence (see Chapters 1, 2 and 3), it can be concluded that a long time before Islam started, these titles were used for the collection of the Judaeo-Christian Scriptures as available today.

If the Gospel and the Torah spoken of by the Qur'an are not the same as the Old and the New Testament (known also as the *Injil* and *Tawrat* among millions of Arabic, Farsi, Urdu and Turkish speaking Christians) and that they did not exist in the same form as in Muhammad's time, then what was the Qur'an referring to? Why did the Qur'an require Christians and Jews to accept the Old and New Testament of Muhammad's time? Why did the Qur'an tell the Jews and Christians to follow their Scriptures if they were not yet in existence or that were only available in corrupted versions? If a Muslim has to believe in the integrity of the Qur'an then he has also to believe that in Muhammad's time the Scriptures of the Jews and Christians existed and that the Qur'an certified their message by saying that they contained guidance and light (Surah 5:47,49). If somehow the author of the Qur'an was doubtful of the integrity of the previous Scriptures, why does it ask both Jews and Christians to follow them in their decisions?

Some Muslims assume that the Qur'an only confirmed and testified to the 'original autographs' of the Torah and the Gospel, although the evidence within the Qur'an itself testifies that it was referring to that which was actually available, there and then, to the Jews and Christians. To confirm and uphold their Scriptures, the Qur'an uses, for example, the following words: *musadiqalima mahum* (confirming what is with them), *musadiqalima baina yadih* (confirming which is between their hands), and *musadiqalima makum* (confirming that which is with them) (Surah 2:41,89; 3:3, 4:47; 5:48; 35:31 and so on).

In the light of the available manuscripts (both incomplete or whole), it can be said with certainty that the Old and the New Testaments of Muhammad's time were exactly the same as available today. Today's Bible translations are based on existing manuscripts that go back even hundreds of years before Muhammad's day. Hence the logic of the Qur'anic verses immediately is that the Injil and Torah as mentioned in the Qur'an are the same as those available to us today in the New Testament and Old Testament of the Bible.

In Judaism, there is a book called 'the Pentateuch' or 'the five books of Moses' which are identical to those in the Bible. These books contain the major part of the Jewish law and are known as the Tawrat/Torah/Law. However, Jews often use the same term to describe the whole collection of books, which Christians call the Old Testament. It is interesting to read in a tradition of Islam that the Torah read by the Jews of Madina also included the book of Isaiah. This indicates that the Qur'an was referring to the *whole* collection of the Jewish Scriptures with the word Torah and not just what was revealed to Moses. For example in the following Islamic tradition transmitted by Bukhari, Darimi and Mishkat:

Ata b. Yasar told that he met Abdullah b. Amr b. al-As and asked him to inform him of the description of God's messenger given in the Torah. He agreed, swearing by God that he was certainly described in the Torah by part of the description of him given in the Qur'an when it says, 'O prophet, We have sent you as a witness, a bearer of good tidings, and a warner, and a guard for the common people. You are my servant and my messenger; I have called you the one who trusts, not harsh or rough, nor loud-voiced in the streets. He will not repulse evil with evil, but will pardon and forgive, and God will not take him till He uses him to straighten the crooked creed so that people may say there is no god but God, and opens thereby blind eyes, deaf ears and hardened hearts.' [6]

The first part of this report is from Surah 33:45 and the later is a paraphrase reminiscent of Isaiah 42:1–4. From these verses, it is obvious that the version of the Torah that the Jews read contained the books of the prophets. The question of whether or not this passage refers to a particular person is not the issue here; it will not be discussed here.

Several narratives of the Gospel?

All the documentary evidence shows that the gospel narratives as found in the New Testament were available in Muhammad's day. Today, we call these four narratives the Gospels, although, at times the title 'Gospel' is used for all the documents, singly and collectively. Long before the time of Muhammad and the Qur'an, the documents were regarded as *the* definitive record of the revelation Jesus showed to the disciples. In the light of available evidence, these documents are the most reliable historical records of

---

[6] Mishkat al.

what the first disciples heard Jesus teach and what they saw him doing.

Ahmad Deedat, a prominent Muslim protagonist, asks, 'The Gospel is a frequently used word, but what Gospel did Jesus preach?'[7] Christians usually answer that the Gospel stands for the good news of the Kingdom of God which Jesus preached (Matthew 24:14). He was telling people that such a Kingdom was near (Matthew 9:35). The only way to join this spiritual kingdom, was to come through Jesus (John 14:4). Christians believe that Jesus gave the good news, which was that he came specifically to give his life for many; he died on the cross to bring about forgiveness; he rose again to demonstrate his victory over death, and he lives to grant assurance of forgiveness and eternal life to whoever believes in him.

Muslims argue that the existence of the four narratives of the *gospel* in the New Testament, is in itself evidence of corruption and unreliability. Christians argue that a more accurate view is that the gospel of Jesus is indeed one, but that 'One' is presented in four ways but, under the guidance of God's Spirit, the message is still one and the same. The Qur'an for example has at least two narratives of Jesus' birth and several narratives of the same stories of Abraham, Adam and Noah within its one collection of the Qur'an. Yet Muslims still treat it as reliable Scripture. Accordingly, it should not be a problem to find four narratives of what Jesus did and said.

Questioning the authenticity of the New Testament, Deedat states: 'In his life time Jesus never wrote a single word, nor did he instruct anyone to do so.'[8] His statement is exaggerated; Jesus could and did write (John 8:6–8). Christians agree that Jesus did not write down the gospel himself but add that if such a charge is

---

[7] Ahmad Deedat, *Is the Bible God's Word?*, p.8.
[8] ibid., p.8.

sufficient to discredit the validity of the Christian Scriptures, then this can also be levelled against Muhammad and the Qur'an. Muhammad did not write nor did he instruct Abu Bakr, Umar and Uthman to collect and compile one official Qur'an. In fact Bukhari states that when Zaid Bin Thabit was asked by Umar and Abu Bakr to collect and compile the first Qur'an, he said, 'How would you do something which Allah's apostle did not do?' It was Abu Bakr, not Muhammad, who replied, 'By Allah, it is a good project.'[9]

It was not so in the case of Jesus and his disciples. Before his crucifixion, Jesus told them that the Holy Spirit would *remind* them of all the things he had said and done implying that they were to propagate his teachings (John 14:26 – 16:13). Just as the Qur'an was collected into a fixed form after Muhammad's death, so the Gospel narratives were put together after Jesus' ascension. If Muhammad's *ashab* (companions), are said to have remembered what he told or narrated to them in order that the Qur'an could be put together afterwards, then it is also possible that the disciples of Jesus remembered what Jesus said, thus explaining why the Gospel is available to us today in its four complementary forms.

It is noteworthy that Jesus promised his disciples that the Holy Spirit would come down and lead them. The Holy Spirit is the reason why the fourfold message of Matthew, Mark, Luke and John came to be accepted by the Church, and why it is still available to us today. No such promise was available to the companions of Muhammad. Furthermore, as mentioned before, the Qur'an testifies that the disciples of Jesus were inspired, while no such facility was known to be available to the disciples of Muhammad when they put together the Qur'an.

---

[9] *Sahih al-Bukhari*, Vol. 6, p.477.

Strictly, these gospels are not called those 'of' Matthew, Mark, Luke and John: in Greek the title is 'the Gospel according to'. It is only for brevity that the shorter title is often employed. So Christians claim that there is indeed one Gospel just as there is one Christ, who claimed that his teaching was from God (John 7:16; 8:28; 12:49,50). Christians also assert that the Gospel relates not only to what Jesus said but also to what he did. The proclamation which led to the conversion of both Jews and Gentiles was the good news that by his death and triumphal resurrection, Jesus had procured remission of sins and opened the kingdom of heaven to all believers.

One Gospel?

The early Christian community could not compile and enforce one official gospel account for posterity, as early Muslims did with the Qur'an. Nor did they burn or dispose of the original scripts of the Gospel with the intention of standardising to one text, as was the case with the Qur'an. Rather these scripts remained as they were; some of them still exist. The false testimony and writings of heretics were and are made available to interested readers to decide for themselves. Most of the false writings and even those treated as 'Apocrypha' (see Appendix) are still around because Christians are sure about the authenticity of the Gospel they have in their possession. Not only this, but when printing was invented, these spurious writings were printed as well, thus giving ample opportunity to compare the contents of these books with the received text of the Bible.

By contrast, we know that the 'false Qur'ans' held by Musailmah and Aswad Ansi were suppressed by the Muslim hierarchy so that they could not be compared with the present Qur'an (See Chapter 9). They and their followers were massacred in battle. Those who remained only saved their lives by accepting the official line. Yet the effect of the teaching of Musailmah was so influential that Ibn Masood found in Kufah a group which still believed in the teaching of Musailmah long after the initial suppression. He quickly consulted the Caliph Uthman who ordered the group to conform or be killed.[10]

There were dissidents among the early Christian community – men like Marcion, Arius and minor groups like the Ebionite and Algio. Each had their own prized collections of Scriptures. In exactly the same way, several companions of Muhammad and their pupils had their own versions of the Qur'an. The *Kharijiah* and, later, other groups of both Shia and Sunni Muslims had differing views not only about the interpretation of the Qur'an but also about its text.

In spite of such differences, if it can be accepted that the great majority of Muslims upheld the text of the Qur'an (and their views are preserved for us today), then the same is also true about Christians who, generation after generation, have upheld the authenticity of the four narratives of the gospel, the authenticity being evidenced by contemporary documents of that era.

Some Muslims argue that the four gospels were only accepted as official in the fourth century by the council of Nicea (325 CE). Christians respond that the council confirmed what the great majority of Christians already believed. They did not invent or select but rather published a formal list of what was already believed by the majority of Christians.

---

[10] Khurshid Ahmad, *Hazrat Uthman ke sarkari Khatoot*, p.139.

The original language of the Gospel

Muslims state that Jesus himself spoke in Aramaic and Hebrew and so did some of his disciples. They say that the Scriptures possessed by Christians today are merely translations of Jesus' words into Greek and other languages. They argue that a translation cannot be accepted as Christ's original words. Translations are not the Word of God. Ajijullah has this to say: 'The books collected into the New Testament do not constitute the utterances of Jesus nor of his disciples. Jesus was a Jew and so were his disciples. If any of Jesus' utterances were to be found preserved in their original form, they could only be in the Hebrew language.'[11]

This statement is completely unsupported by any evidence. Incidentally, Ajijullah also copied a whole chapter in his book, word for word and without any acknowledgement from a prominent Ahmadiyya writer, once the head of this sect of Islam.[12] The Ahmadiyya sect is considered to be heretical by other Muslims. Nevertheless, his plagiarism does not seem to affect the point put forward by Muslims.

Jesus is likely to have spoken Aramaic as his normal everyday language. After having being brought up in Galilee, a region which was thoroughly permeated by Greek influence, he must have communicated in Greek as well. For example, Sepphoris, the capital of Galilee, was only six kilometres from Nazareth or one and a half hours walking distance from where Jesus was brought up. Sepphoris, with its 25,000 inhabitants, was a profoundly

---

[11]   Ajijullah, *Myth of the Cross*, p.85.

[12]   Ajijullah, *Myth of the Cross*, pp.85–88; 114–126; 133–138;140. Compare with Bashiruddin Mahmood Ahmad, *Introduction to the Study of the Holy Qur'an*, pp.47–51; 59–68; 17–19,7; 30–31,37,40,44; 46–47.

Hellenized place. There are contemporary inscriptions and a magnificent theatre capable of seating an audience of 5000 was built there when Jesus was a young man. Not only in this theatre but all over Palestine, plays were performed in the Greek language.[13]

Jesus in such a situation must have frequently encountered Greek-speaking people as he travelled around. There are inscriptions found in Galilee and elsewhere in Palestine which demonstrate that Greek was used even by orthodox Jews in the synagogues and on their tombstones. Even in the temple of Jerusalem Greek script was used on the 'Stone of forbidding'.

In the light of the New Testament, it is fairly obvious that Jesus' first language was Aramaic. He was also able to speak and read Hebrew which is evident from Luke 4:16–30, where he reads from a scroll of Isaiah and then interprets the text for the audience. However, as we have seen, there are reasons for believing that, at times, Jesus also spoke Greek. Mark 7:24–30 refers to his meeting with a Syro-Phoenician woman. She was clearly Greek and would in all probability not have been able to speak in Aramaic or Hebrew. Perhaps that is the reason why Mark 7:26 points out that the woman was Greek-speaking and it is reasonable to assume that the conversation with Jesus was conducted in Greek. Jesus also talked with Pontius Pilate whose languages were Greek and Latin. Here too, it is reasonable to assume that Jesus spoke Greek.

After his resurrection, when Jesus talked with Peter at the lakeside to test his continuing love, the structure of the dialogue and the sentences show the use of rhyme and exploit the shades of meaning in the Greek words for 'love', 'know' and 'feed' which could not have had the same effect in Aramaic or Hebrew. Peter and Andrew

---

[13] Carsten Peter Thiede, Contributor to *Jesus 2000*, p.25.

themselves have names of Greek origin. So although the
Gospels were written down in common Greek and not
Hebrew or Aramaic, this is mainly because in most
instances it would have been the language actually used
by Jesus himself.

Even if it is accepted that Jesus spoke only Aramaic or
Hebrew and that his words were put into Greek at a later
date, and even if it is then said that a translation is inher-
ently unreliable, even then the same concern can be used
against the Qur'an. For in it there are verses in Arabic
which are said to be the words of Jesus (Surah 3:49–54;
5:114–118; 61:14 etc.). Now, if Jesus' words can be recorded
as the word of God in Arabic, a translation, why can't his
words be recorded in the Greek language of the Christian
Scriptures?

Not only that, but one may also find words spoken by
various prophets in the Qur'an. Most of these prophets
spoke Hebrew but their words are again recorded in Arabic
in the Qur'an. So one can see that Muslims don't have these
people's original words either. If such a situation does not
affect the integrity of the Qur'an, then neither can it be
treated as evidence to question the integrity of the Bible.

The spread of the Pauline Gospel

Many Muslims believe that the present teaching of
Christianity is the work of the apostle Paul. They claim
that it was Paul who created his own version of the
Christian faith at the expense of those whom Jesus had
chosen.[14] There was a struggle between Pauline and
Judaeo-Christianity[15] and eventually Pauline Christianity

[14] Rahmatullah, *Izharul Haqq*, part III, p.30 (Editor's note);
Maurice Bucaille, *The Bible, the Qur'an and Science*, p.52.
[15] Ajijullah, *Myth of the Cross*, p.85–87.

triumphed. Perhaps it 'won' because it was more attractive having incorporated some pagan ideas. According to this theory, the struggle started when a disagreement took place between Paul and Peter and between Barnabas and Paul (Galatians 2:1–16; Acts 21:17–20).

Certainly the Scriptures do mention an occasion when there was a confrontation where Paul rebuked Peter. The argument was in fact about a minor aspect of the old Mosaic law and not about the major doctrines that Christianity today stands for. Anyway, we know that the matter was soon resolved because Peter and Paul were soon friends again and in complete agreement, so much so that we later find another passage where Peter calls Paul 'our dear brother' (2 Peter 3:15–16). With regard to the disagreement between Paul and Barnabas, see Chapter 7.

The companions of Muhammad also had arguments and differences with each other on religious matters. Some were very serious, such as the dispute between Uthman and Ibn Masood concerning the compilation of the Qur'an by Zaid Bin Thabit. The situation flared up to the extent that Uthman, then the caliph, had Ibn Masood thrown out of the mosque and threatened him with excommunication (see Chapter 4).

If such a situation is not a proof of Uthman establishing his brand of Islam and the text of Qur'an by force, then the two occasions of minor disagreements between Paul and Peter and Barnabas should not be a problem either. It is true that the history of Christianity does show how Christians differed and had disagreements with each other. Their example is no different from Muslims, however, in that some sects of Islam who had differences actually fought each other. As the majority of Muslims believe, their quarrels did not affect the integrity of the message of the Qur'an, so the same can be said about the Bible.

There is no basis in history for the idea that there was a struggle between Paul's group and the true disciples of Jesus, that the true disciples lost, and that only Pauline teaching prevailed. Such an idea is even against the Islamic Scripture. The Qur'an describes a struggle between believers and unbelievers but states that God gave power to true believers in Jesus against their enemies. God gave them victory and so they became dominant (Surah 61:14).

In another Surah, the Qur'an states that the People of the Book had a division among themselves; they fought each other and among them there were those who ignored a part of what was revealed. They placed enmity and hatred between others but true believers continued in their faith and succeeded (Surah 42:13,14; 2:253; 5:15,16; 61:14). In none of these verses does it say that 'unbelieving Christians' changed the Bible or that they gained victory over true Christians as some Muslims would like to believe. This is not only historically false but it also directly contradicts the teaching of the Qur'an.

Isnad, a chain of transmission

Some Muslims see the Bible as being akin to their collections of traditions, *Hadith*. However, not finding records of a chain of witnesses, known as *isnad*, to the authenticity of the reports, they reject it. For example, to disprove the authenticity of the gospel narratives, Rahmatullah quotes Imam Al-Qurtubi by saying, 'the present gospels have not been authenticated by means of an unbroken chain of transmission'.[16] In their discussions with Christians, Muslims sometimes ask to see proof of such a chain to

---

[16] Rahmatullah, part III, pp.37, 41.

substantiate the sayings and deeds of Jesus that are recorded.[17]

First of all, *Isnad* is not a requirement that Jesus put on Christians nor does the Bible depend on the Islamic method of traditions and transmitters. In a sense this aspect of transmission is well covered by the writings of the early Church fathers. Since the 1800s many manuscripts and other archaeological evidence have come to light which further reinforce the integrity of what is found in the Scriptures.

Secondly, *Isnad*, is not necessarily the complete antidote to doubt. Muslims believe that they have unbroken chains of transmission concerning the textual collections of what Muhammad said and did. However, the most authentic collections along with the names of their transmitters were committed to writing only after a period of about two hundred and fifty years after Muhammad's death. During that period, so Muslim historians tell us, many spurious collections came to the fore. Thousands of traditions were invented to bolster spurious reports each with a perfect chain containing the names of transmitters reaching all the way up to a companion of Muhammad.[18] Some (but not all) were detected and the authors punished, but there was no reliable test available to show which texts were right and which were spurious. People like Ibn Abi Awja (d.772) admitted inventing and putting into circulation about four thousand traditions with perfect unbroken chains of transmitters right back to Muhammad's lifetime.[19]

---

[17] Izzat, p.4; Rahmatullah, part I, pp. 18–19.

[18] *Ibn Khaliqan*, Vol 1, p.590 as cited by Hughes, *Dictionary of Islam*, p.639.

[19] Macdonald, *The Development of Muslim Theology, Jurisprudence and Constitutional Theory*, p.80.

Ahadith, traditions, still include many reports which can be called into question.[20] The most reliable authority among the transmitters is Abu Hurrairah. He accepted Islam just three years before Muhammad died. There are more than 5,000[21] reports from him covering just over a thousand days, although a number of them contradict each other. Muslim scholars are not sure whether he himself fabricated any *Hadith* or material was falsely attributed to him at a later date. Another example is Abdallah Ibn Abbas who was 13 years old when Muhammad died and yet more than 1600 traditions bear his name as the transmitter. Muslim scholars do recognise that much of what has been attributed to him must have been forged by later narrators.[22] So one can see that *Isnad*, the chain of transmitters, is no guarantee of the quality of the evidence either.

We see that Muslims have adopted a standard which even the Qur'an cannot reach. They do not have an unbroken and reliable chain of transmission for each of the Qur'an's revelations. They have to rely on the evidence provided by a secondary source, namely *Ahadith* which were collected much later. Even the information provided in the *Ahadith* is open to question. If, in spite of this situation Muslims can accept the validity of the Qur'an, it seems illogical to question the Christian Scriptures, of which many early copies are available. Seeing these copies, one is reminded that the weakest ink is stronger than the best memory.

---

[20] Muhammad Zubayr Siddiqi, *Hadith Literature*, pp.58–60.
[21] Fatimah Mernissi, *Women and Islam: An Historical and Theological Enquiry*, p.80.
[22] Muhammad Zubayr Siddiqi, *Hadith Literature*, pp.20–22.

Asatir ul Awalin, stories of times gone by

Some Muslims claim that the present Torah is just a book of stories which have no truth in them. They refer to the Pentateuch, the five books of Moses (Genesis, Exodus, Leviticus, Numbers and Deuteronomy) and dispute whether these are in fact the books of Moses. They allege that these writings are 'a collection of stories and traditions which were current among Jews and written down by their scholars without a critical view to their authority.'[23] Some question: 'How can Muslims take the Bible as divine revelation when all it contains is the work (reports, stories, myths) of groups of people?'[24]

It is certainly true that the Bible does contain reports and stories, in particular the history of how God chose a nation, the Israelites, sent his prophets among them, and prepared the way for Jesus to be the saviour of all the people of the earth. The Qur'an also contains reports, stories and part of the history of the Israelites and the people in Arabia. It has stories of the prophets and the Israelites in such detail that the Qur'an itself says that the Makkans sarcastically started calling it *asatir ul awalin*, the stories of people gone by.

If the Torah is not inspired and the books included in it only contain a collection of stories and traditions, why then does the Qur'an refer to it and even quote from it? The story of creation; the fall of Adam and Eve; the story of Noah and his ark; Abraham; Isaac; Lot; Jacob; Joseph and Moses; David, Solomon and Jesus are also found in the Qur'an. The story of Moses, his discourses with Pharaoh and the exodus of the Israelites are mentioned in several places in the Qur'an. We find that the Qur'an has borrowed material not only from the first five books of Moses but also in several places from the rest of the Old

---

[23] Rahmatullah, *Izharul Haqq*, Part I, p.22.

[24] Izzat and Abu, p.6. Text and parentheses *sic*.

Testament although in a fragmentary manner. Muhammad himself had to admit that the Qur'an 'is in the Scriptures of the ancients' (Surah 26:196).

Moreover, the 28th Surah is named *al-Qasas*, the story. If, according to Muslims, the text of the Bible is indeed described by critics as myths and fables which need a lot of explanation, then the Qur'an is no different because, like the Bible, it also contains passages that are hard to explain. Talking birds, talking ants and giants of the jinns, or the instantaneous transport of the throne of Sheba are found in only a few verses of the Qur'an (Surah 27:15–44).

As Muslims struggle for explanations of certain texts of the Qur'an, so do Christians struggle over some texts of the Bible. If the stories, histories and the work of people groups do not affect the reliability of the Qur'an then how is it that the Bible is declared unreliable? Both books and the explanations of their adherents should be weighed with the same balance.

Pagan origins

Some Muslims link the teachings of the Bible with polytheistic pagan sources in an attempt to prove that the Qur'an does not refer to the Scriptures as available to Christians today.[25] They compare the Christian feasts of Easter and Christmas[26] with pagan practices such as Easter eggs and Christmas trees while others go further comparing Christian beliefs with ancient myths, thus concluding that these similarities prove that Christianity is founded on pagan rites and creeds.[27]

---

[25] Kamal-ud-Din, *The Sources of Christianity*, p.15.
[26] Izzat Khan, pp.18–20.
[27] Aziz-us-Samad, *A Comparative Study of Christianity and Islam*, p.71.

There is no evidence in history that the early Church was charged with incorporating pagan myths. 'In fact the early Church refused to make room for pagan rites and ceremonies. For example, the Church at Colossae was surrounded by a pagan philosophy that involved a religious life of observing the movements of the stars, which were associated with the powers of the angels and were therefore worshipped.'[28] Instead of harmonising with such practices the Church was warned of this dangerous situation and was called not to participate in any pagan rites or idol feasts (1 Corinthians 10:20–21; Colossians 2:8).

One author, Kamal-ud-Din, in his book, *The Sources of Christianity*, tried to trace Jesus' teachings to pagan origins. Another writer, Abdul Haque, in his book, *Muhammad in World Scriptures*, endeavoured to find similarities between Muhammad and pagan gods to prove the universality of Muhammad. The first writer tries to prove paganism, saying that the story of Jesus in the Bible is an exact copy of the story of Horus, the 'sun-god'.[29] Conversely, the second writer presents a series of similarities between Horus and Muhammad to prove that the former foretold the latter – which, apparently, is *not* paganism![30]

These illustrations show how some writers are unjustified in attempting to discredit the Bible. There is no substance in their argument that Christianity is based on pagan origins. On the contrary, it is easier to say that it is Islam itself which has embarrassing parallels with the various pagan religions preceding it. If Christianity can be accused of following paganism just because it latterly celebrates Good Friday and Easter Sunday 'after the movements of the moon'[31] then the same can be said of Islam

---

[28] Masood, *Jesus and the Indian Messiah*, p.113.
[29] Kamal-ud-Din, *The Sources of Christianity*, p.35.
[30] Abdul Haque, *Muhammad in World Scriptures*, Vol.1, p.395.
[31] Masood, *Jesus and the Indian Messiah*, p.114.

because the dates for Ramadhan and Eid festivals are fixed in the same manner.

Following the method used by Muslims, one can list various beliefs and practices of Islam to suggest the incorporation of Zoroastrian, Sabaean or pagan Arab traditions. For instance, Islamic prayer and fasting parallels that of the Sabaeans who performed prayers seven times a day and five of these prayers were at the same hours as those of Islam. They fasted for thirty days and observed *Eid* festivals, and venerated the *Ka'ba,* the cube-like building in the centre of the sacred mosque at Makkah.

Similarly, the incident of *Miraj* – the ascent of Muhammad to heaven and the passing visit to hell and paradise may be found in ancient Zoroastrian tales dating some four hundred years before the time of Muhammad.[32] However, if such similarities do not mean that Islam has its origin in pre-Islamic sources, then one should not use the same yardstick when looking at the Bible.

Calamities

To prove that Muhammad's contemporaries were reading something other than the present collection of the Bible, some Muslims argue that the Judaeo-Christian Scriptures were destroyed during the hard times Christians faced in the first three hundred years of their history.[33] However, this argument flies in the face of the available evidence. It is true that Christians were persecuted and many copies of their Scriptures were destroyed, but the evidence in libraries shows that many copies survived. The discoveries made since 1800 and, most recently, the Dead Sea Scrolls speak for themselves. The Israelites

---

[32] Tisdall, *The Original Sources of the Qur'an*, pp.79–81, 230.
[33] Izzat Khan, p.4.

were, from time to time, subjected to persecution by foreign kingdoms. Instead of being wiped out or assimilated, they survived while, one after the other, most of the national groups around them disappeared from the world scene. Similarly, the Hebrew Scriptures survived and, when Jesus came, he testified to their validity and truth as is apparent in the New Testament section of the Bible.

Christians were indeed an oppressed group for quite a long time. The Jewish authorities in Jerusalem and Palestine tried to suppress them at home and tried their best to stop their work in other parts of the Roman Empire, as is obvious from New Testament history (Acts 5:27,28; 7:58–60; 11:19–21; 13:45; 14:19; 18:5,6).

During the time of the emperor Nero, the initially tolerant attitude of the Roman authorities changed. Being a Christian became a capital offence. People like Tacitus boasted of the tortures inflicted on Christians. In the year 303 the emperor Diocletian initiated the more severe persecution of Christians. To stamp out Christianity, he ordered that their Scriptures should be burned. Though many atrocities were committed, Christians and their Scriptures could not be wiped out. The next ten years also saw the beginning of the downfall of paganism in the Roman Empire as well. In fact Christianity spread more rapidly under persecution than before. Fresh evidence of this same effect was found recently in communist countries where Christian belief spread more vibrantly under persecution. Therefore to say that the Scriptures of the people of the Book disappeared is without any evidence at all. The Qur'an itself makes it clear that people were reading the pre-Islamic Scriptures in the seventh century. How could they read and find guidance in them if they were already lost during the persecution period? Much more mysterious is the lack of Qur'anic copies from the 1st period of Muslim expansion.

Conclusion

By analysing a few specific objections and comments, it is shown that the critical attitude of some Muslims towards the Judaeo-Christian Scriptures is groundless. If the same standards by which they measure the Bible (and find it lacking) are applied to the Qur'an, then the same result is obtained. After considering and taking note of each aspect of the Bible that is criticised by Muslims, it is concluded that the Bible as we have it today is indeed the same as the Judaeo-Christian Scriptures which were available at the time of Muhammad and which the Qur'an confirms, and declares to be *huddan lin-nas*, a guidance for people.

Questions concerning the Gospel of Barnabas

And when Jesus, son of Mary said, 'O children of Israel, I am the messenger of Allah unto you, confirming that which was revealed before me in Torah, and bringing good tidings of a messenger who cometh after me, whose name is the "Praised One".' (Surah 61:6)

Muslims who read and recite this verse in the Qur'an, work backwards to decide what they think the 'original Gospel' must have said. They claim that it would have clearly predicted the coming of Muhammad. It could not have called Jesus the Son of God and must have denied the death of Jesus by crucifixion. In their efforts to discredit the Christian Scriptures, some Muslims look for documents which may fit their argument, no matter if these have been declared spurious by the whole Christian Church. One such document is the so-called 'Gospel of Barnabas'. In this 'gospel', as some Muslims claim, there is much which contradicts the canonical gospels but does fit in with Muslim beliefs. In their discussions with Christians, they go so far as to claim this gospel to be the original gospel that descended upon Jesus from heaven and which he dictated to Barnabas. Some Muslims base their presentation of the life and teaching of Jesus upon this document, rather than on the Qur'an, the Bible or the traditions.

A Pakistani Muslim, Ataur Rahim who took great pains to introduce this 'gospel' into Pakistan had this to say:

> The gospel of Barnabas is the only known surviving gospel written by a disciple of Jesus, that is by a man who spent most of his time in the actual company of Jesus during the three years in which he was delivering his message. Therefore he had direct experience and knowledge of Jesus' teaching, unlike all the authors of the four accepted Gospels.[1]

He totally ignores the fact that John was a disciple from the beginning and Matthew a little later. He offers no evidence that Barnabas was a disciple *during* Jesus' three year ministry. Another Muslim, Ali Akbar made the following comments:

> Christians do not regard the gospel of St. Barnabas as an integral part of the New Testament and it is not often preached in their churches. This Gospel was condemned by the Christian council three hundred years before the prophet Muhammad. The reason for this is, no doubt, that the advent of the prophet Muhammad is predicted therein in very clear words.[2]

No evidence of this book being mentioned at any Christian council is given. Similar claims are made by Abdu L-Ahad Dawud in his popular book, *Muhammad in the Bible*:

> This Gospel has been rejected by Churches because its language is more in accordance with the revealed Scriptures and because it is very expressive and explicit about the nature of

---

[1] Rahim, *Jesus: A prophet of Islam*, p.37.

[2] Akbar, *Israel and the Prophecies of the Qur'an*, p.6.

Jesus Christ's mission, and above all because it records the exact words of Jesus concerning Muhammad.[3]

What is the truth? Why do Christians reject this gospel? Is it because this gospel has certain alleged prophecies about Muhammad or because they have more solid arguments against the credibility of this document?

Background of this gospel

Muslims first became aware of the existence of this gospel through the work of George Sale who mentioned it in his translation of the Qur'an into English in 1734. In his preface, Sale mentions a Spanish version written by a Mostafa de Aranda, who claimed to have translated it from Italian. It was alleged that an Italian Christian monk, Fra Marino, had *stolen* it from the library of Pope Sixtus V (1585–1590) while the pope was asleep in his library and that Marino became a Muslim after reading it.[4] This translation has somehow perished, although various fragments of the Spanish text are still available. The Italian version found its way to Holland and was found in 1709 in the possession of J.F. Cramer, a councillor to the King of Prussia (Germany). He, in 1713, gave it to Prince Eugene of Savoy and over the next few years it passed from one hand to another until it reached Vienna in 1738 and was deposited in the Imperial Library where it stays to this day.[5]

Lonsdale and Laura Ragg were responsible for translating it into English and printing it in 1907 with 70 pages of introduction giving convincing reasons why various scholars believed that this was a fake Gospel written in the

---

[3] Abdu L-Ahad Dawud, *Muhammad in the Bible*, p.89.

[4] Sale, George, *Preliminary Discourse to the Koran*, pp. ix–x & 58.

[5] Barnabas-Evangeliums, Codex No. 2662, Handschriften-und Inkunabelsammlung, Austria National Library, Vienna.

Middle Ages. In 1908, an Arabic translation with a new introduction was published in Cairo and in 1916 two Urdu editions were published, which were based on the Arabic version.

Between 1960 and 1980, translations of this gospel appeared in many of the languages of the Muslim majority countries. The reprinting, in Pakistan in 1973, of the English translation by Lonsdale and Laura Ragg was much publicised by Islamic Missions.[6] Their Urdu and English presses promoted it and Muslim religious leaders introduced it as the true Gospel of Jesus.[7] The same year, a new Urdu translation was published by *Jama'at-e-Islami*, Lahore, with an introduction by the founder of the organisation, Maulana Abul Ala Mawdudi.[8]

Both the English and Urdu translations were reprinted several times. By 1990 there were 203,000 English copies printed by one publisher alone, Aisha Bawany, in Pakistan. The interesting thing is that none of these reprints included the 70 pages of introduction by Lonsdale and Laura Ragg, because in their introduction they provide evidence to the effect that the book is a medieval forgery. The facsimile of the original title page, in some of the English editions, gives the misleading impression that one is dealing with the complete text of the original book by Lonsdale and Laura Ragg. The English translation of the document has now been printed by several Muslim publishers in Britain and America without any

---

[6]   Rahim, M A, *The Gospel of Barnabas* (Qur'an Council of Pakistan, Karachi, 1973).

[7]   *The Gospel of Barnabas*, 3rd Edition, with introduction (Begum Aisha Bawany Wakf. 1974); *The Gospel of Barnabas*, 6th Edition, with appendix (Begum Aisha Bawany Wakf. 1977).

[8]   *Barnabas ki Injil* (Islamic Publications Ltd. Lahore. 1974), Asi Zia-ai, *Barnabas ki Injil* (Islamic Publications Ltd. Lahore) 3rd Edition, 1981.

acknowledgement to previous publishers or to Lonsdale and Laura Ragg, the translators into English.

The content of this gospel

The gospel of Barnabas can be divided into several sections of which the following is a brief description:

Chapters 1–9:
>The birth of Jesus; his childhood and his 'disputation' with the doctors concerning the law.

Chapters 10–47:
>Jesus receives a book, the *Injil* from God. He begins his ministry and performs miracles. He preaches, *'I am not the messiah, the messiah will be born of the Ishmaelites'*.

Chapters 48–98:
>The Roman soldiers worship him as God but Jesus tells them that he is not the son of God. He has come to give the glad tidings of the coming of Muhammad.

Chapters 99–126:
>A crowd gathers to appoint Jesus as king but Jesus leaves for Damascus and then travels to some other cities.

Chapters 127–153:
>Jesus teaches his disciples about penitence, fasting, prayer, fear of God and high morals.

Chapters 154–191:
>Jesus teaches about the sinful world, the nature of sin, restoration, freedom, paradise and predestination. A scribe is also mentioned who claims that he saw a secret book of Moses which declares that the 'Messiah springeth from Ishmael and not from Isaac'.

Chapters 192–222:
> Jesus raises Lazarus from the dead and predicts
> the judgement of Jerusalem. The Jews attempt to
> stone him but he vanishes. He is betrayed by
> Judas. Jesus is taken into heaven and Judas' face is
> made to look like that of Jesus. Judas is mistakenly
> crucified in place of Jesus. Jesus appears to his
> friends and his mother and tells them that he was
> not crucified. He charges Barnabas to write the
> gospel *(Injil)* after which he returns to heaven.

The message of this gospel

Muslims value this gospel highly because it teaches
against the doctrine presented in the New Testament. The
following are the main points of this gospel which may
affirm some of the Muslim beliefs but contradicts the
teaching of the New Testament:

1. Jesus is a servant and only a messenger of God
   (Barnabas, chapter 55). He is not God, nor the Son
   of God, nor a god (Barnabas, chapters 53 and 100).
2. Jesus predicts the coming of the Messiah who is
   Muhammad (Barnabas, chapters 42–44). He himself refuses to be a messiah but gives this title to
   Muhammad. It was Ishmael who was to be sacrificed, not Isaac (Barnabas, chapter 44).
3. Jesus ascended to heaven before the crucifixion
   and Judas was made to look like Jesus (Barnabas,
   chapter 220). Jesus did not die on the cross (Barnabas, chapter 215). It was Judas Iscariot who died on
   the cross (Barnabas, chapter 216). The disciples
   stole the body of Judas and claimed that Jesus was
   risen. Many of the disciples have taught this
   deception, including Paul.

The writer of this gospel

Was Barnabas the writer of this gospel? Muslims say, 'yes' to this question and call upon the book of Acts for evidence where Barnabas is mentioned. However our investigation reveals that the Barnabas of Acts and the Barnabas of this gospel are two different people who lived at different times.

According to the New Testament, Barnabas was not present during the ministry of Jesus. He is first mentioned in Acts *after* the church was already established. He, like other disciples, sold his property to raise money for distribution to the poor (Acts 4). He was a Jew from Cyprus named Joseph whom the apostles called Bar-nabas, which means 'son of encouragement' (Acts 4:36).

According to the document in question, however, Barnabas was an apostle of Jesus and known by this name throughout Jesus' ministry. On many occasions Jesus is reported to have called him Barnabas instead of Joseph. This weakens the credibility of this gospel because Barnabas was never called to be an apostle by Jesus, according to all the available lists in the other Gospels. Christians reject the authorship of Barnabas of the New Testament for these additional reasons.

The Barnabas of this gospel rejects the deity of Christ. Jesus is alleged to have denied being equal with God and to have claimed that he was only a messenger and servant of God. However, in the New Testament in Acts, Barnabas was the one who introduced Paul to the apostles at Jerusalem and encouraged them to trust him. The first thing Paul had preached after his conversion was that Jesus was the Son of God (Acts 9:20) and no doubt Barnabas was well aware of it. If Paul was preaching something unacceptable would Barnabas not have called for him to be silenced rather than fighting for his acceptance as a preacher of God's word?

This Gospel denounces the teaching of Paul regarding circumcision, the crucifixion, the death and resurrection of Jesus. However, the book of Acts shows that Paul and Barnabas had a joint ministry for one full year. They both preached the same thing concerning Jesus' resurrection and his deity (Acts 13:33). Here, Barnabas along with Paul can be seen in debate with some who insisted on circumcision. This debate was not between Paul and Barnabas but between the people from Judea on the one side and Paul and Barnabas on the other (Acts 15). Thus it is illogical to accept that the Barnabas of the New Testament is responsible for a document that rejects the very teachings he proclaimed and defended.

Muslims quote from Galatians 2:13 and Acts 15:38–40 as proof that there was a disagreement on doctrinal matters between Paul and Barnabas. According to the first reference Barnabas was reprimanded for religious discrimination. Just to avoid offending some Jewish Christians, Barnabas and Peter did not sit at a meal with Gentile converts. Paul censured this behaviour. Acts 15:2 shows that Peter and Barnabas later realised their error and accepted Paul's argument. Muslims may ask, 'Was not the root problem an issue of doctrine, namely, justification by faith, not by observing the works of the law, as the rest of Galatians chapter 2 reveals?' The answer is that although it is a doctrinal issue, it does not leave Paul in the wrong. Also, 1 Corinthians 9:6 which was written after the split, shows that Paul and Barnabas were back on good terms again. We should appreciate that the split reported in Galatians chapter 2 was short-lived.

The case in Acts 15:38–40 relates how Paul did not want to take John Mark with them on their next journey because he remembered how John Mark had abandoned them in

Pamphilia in the middle of the first journey (Acts 12:12; 13:13). Paul was concerned that John Mark might do the same again and cause further problems. Later, however, the same Paul commends John Mark in his letters and expresses his need for him in his ministry (Colossians 4:10; 2 Timothy 4:11).

The evidence reveals that the dispute here was a *personal* matter and not doctrinal. There is no evidence that Paul and Barnabas had split because of a doctrinal clash. In fact the investigation in this case convinces us of the unity between these two men rather than discord.

So why should Barnabas suddenly change his belief? Muslims offer rather fanciful explanations. A favourite theory, for example, is offered by Rahim, who tried his best to propagate this gospel with great zeal in Pakistan and wrote about the life of Jesus as portrayed in this gospel. He says:

> Paul was a Roman citizen. He must have learned the language of Rome. He probably spoke Greek as it was the official language of the area in which he was born. The epistles he later wrote to the Christian communities in Greece must have been written in their native language. This meant he could travel in Greece and probably Italy without any language difficulty. Barnabas, on the other hand spoke neither of the two languages. John Mark, who spoke Greek, had accompanied him on the first missionary journey into Greece, to act as his interpreter. If Barnabas was to go there by himself, he would not be able to make himself understood. Thus Paul's refusal to travel with Mark may have been a roundabout way of ensuring that Barnabas would refuse to travel with him.[9]

---

[9] Rahim, *Jesus: A Prophet of Islam*, p.63.

His statement is riddled with unsupported claims, many
of which are easily refuted. The conclusion cannot hope to
be valid on such defective premises. It is also inconsistent
with the statement in the same book that Barnabas was
born in Cyprus. His native tongue would therefore have
been Greek and the argument is rendered invalid by his
own words. Also, Rahim says that Paul and Barnabas
were fellow students under Gamaliel. If such were the
case, this would mean that both were educated men who
had learned the teaching of the Old Testament and the traditions. The Old Testament was translated into Greek in
250 BCE, making it available to the Greek-speaking world.
If it was so important that there was a need for a translation into Greek three hundred years *before* Barnabas and
Paul, how much greater would be the need of the Greek-
speaking Jewish scholars who lived in 30–40 CE? Evidently then, being an educated Jew, Barnabas would not
need an interpreter. He would have fully understood
what Paul and the other apostles were preaching. Hence
there would be no conflict or misunderstanding regarding the deity of Christ, his crucifixion, resurrection and
ascension.

Evidence from history

Christians claim that this gospel did not exist during the
time of the apostles, their pupils, the church fathers or
their pupils. Almost every book of the New Testament is
mentioned and quoted in the writings of the early Christians but no reference whatever is made to this work.
However, Muslims claim a long, colourful history for this
manuscript going back to Irenaeus (130–200). For example
Rahim says that Irenaeus 'quoted extensively from the
Gospel of Barnabas in support of his views. This shows

that the Gospel of Barnabas was in circulation in the first and second centuries of Christianity.'[10] On examination one finds that Irenaeus in his writings quoted from the *Epistle* of Barnabas and not from what Rahim calls the Gospel of Barnabas. (An 'Epistle' is a letter and usually explains doctrine, while a 'Gospel' is an account of Jesus' life).

Rahim claimed that during Emperor Zeno's rule in 478, the remains of Barnabas were discovered, and a copy of the Gospel of Barnabas, written by his own hand, was found on his breast. According to him it is recorded in the Acta Sanctorium, Boland Junii, Tome 2, pages 422–450, published in Antwerp in 1698.[11] However, the record actually says that a copy of the gospel according to Matthew, copied by Barnabas himself, written in his own hand, was found on his breast. This deliberate alteration of the record reflects little credit on Rahim's integrity. He omitted the words 'according to Matthew, copied by Barnabas himself' and instead inserted 'Gospel of Barnabas'.

Evidence from Muslim history

Since the evidence from Christian history regarding the Gospel of Barnabas is sometimes rejected by Muslims, we now refer to the evidence from Islamic history. The study of Muslim traditions and Muslim historical accounts suggest that Muhammad, the prophet of Islam, had good relations with the Christian ruler at Najran. At the time of Muhammad's birth, Arabs were in contact with Christians in Abyssinia, and also with the three major sections of the Church in the Middle East i.e. Byzantine, Nestorian

---

[10] *The Gospel of Barnabas*, p.xv, (Lahore, Islamic Publications, 1982).

[11] Rahim, *Jesus: A Prophet of Islam*, p.37.

and Jacobite-Monophysites. The Nestorians exercised the most influence over the Arabs. According to Ibn Ishaq, pictures of Mary and Jesus were to be seen on one of the Ka'ba walls.[12]

Muslim traditions tell us about various Christian delegations that came to visit Muhammad for discussion. On one occasion, a group of sixty people headed by Abd al-Masih, bishop of the Najran Christians, met Muhammad in the mosque at Madina to discuss the deity of Christ. Muhammad related to them that Jesus was not God. The incident is said to be recorded in the Qur'an (Surah 3:40–70). Here was an excellent opportunity to mention the gospel of Barnabas as evidence against the Christian claim, if it was in existence, but not so. Neither did Allah reveal to Muhammad any verse with regard to it.

John of Damascus (d.753), known as Yahya b. Mansur, the son of a civil servant who had been a treasurer to Caliph Muawiya and Abdul Malik, wrote on many subjects including the deity of Christ. Surely he would have also mentioned this gospel if it had been in existence then?

Bishop Timotheos (d.823), whose term of office spans the high point of Abbasid power at Baghdad under Harun al-Rashid (786–809), held debates in the court of Khalifa Musa al-Hadi (785–6). Discussions were held not only in defence of what was held to be Islamic orthodoxy against free thinkers and heretics, but also about the four gospels. However, according to the transcripts, nobody mentioned the gospel of Barnabas. Muslim scholars debated the Godhead and the person of Jesus, yet they never mentioned this gospel. Caliph Jafar al-Mutawakal (847–861), who abolished the right of religion and the construction of churches and introduced discriminating laws against

---

[12] Ibn Hisham: *Sira* (trans.), Guilliam, *The Life of Muhammad*, p.552.

Christians and Jews,[13] held debates in his court with people like Bishop Elijah. However, again, no one suggested the gospel of Barnabas as a reference.

The book *Al-Fihrist* of Abu al-Faraj Muhammad ibn Ishaq al-Nadim (935–990), which is claimed by Muslims to deal with every phase of medieval culture, has long lists of books and authors. He gives a list of writings that are part of the Bible but nowhere mentions the so-called gospel of Barnabas.[14]

For several centuries Muslims ruled Spain (756–1492 CE) and there were many dialogues between Muslims and Christians, yet no Muslim ever presented this gospel as evidence against orthodox Christian belief. In this period there were Muslim writers, historians and philosopher like al-Farabi (d.950), al-Masudi (d.956), al-Kindi (d.961), Ibn Hazm (d.1063), al-Ghazali (d.1111), Abu al-Abbas al-Arif (d.1141); Ibn Rushd (d.1198), Muhyi'l Din Ibn al-Arabi (d.1240), and Ibn Khaldun (d.1406). However not one of them mentioned this document. Furthermore, in none of the commentaries on the Qur'an, prior to 1700 CE can any reference to this gospel be found. Therefore it is extremely difficult to believe that this gospel could possibly have been in existence before this time, as discussed below.

Evidence from the document

The physical appearance of the manuscript of the Gospel of Barnabas in existence today suggests, in terms of its binding, the style of writing and its language, that it was written between 1500 and 1590.

---

[13] H. U. Rahman, *A Chronology of Islamic History*, p.188.
[14] *The Fihrist of al-Nadim*, Vol. 1, pp.40–46.

Let us consider first the evidence within the text. In the Torah, God ordered the Israelites to observe a Jubilee year. 'A Jubilee shall that fiftieth year be to you' (Leviticus 25:11). However the gospel of Barnabas mentions this Jubilee but gives the interval of one hundred years (Barnabas, chapter 82). Where did the author get this figure from?

Around the year 1300, Pope Boniface VIII decreed the one hundred year interval for the church. In 1343, Pope Clemens VI changed it back to fifty years and later Pope Paul II (1464–1471) reduced it to twenty-five years. It would appear that the writer knew about the decree of Pope Boniface but thought it had been instituted by Jesus. This compels us to think that this gospel cannot be dated earlier than 1300 CE.

One finds several quotations of the writer Dante are attributed to Jesus in this gospel. For example, Dante's expression, 'false and lying gods' in chapters 23, 78, 217 is not found in the Bible nor in the Qur'an, but shows up only in this gospel. The description of hell in this gospel is also remarkably similar to Dante's fantasy about hell, purgatory and paradise. In its chapter 178, this gospel tells us that there are nine heavens, again reminiscent of Dante. It is interesting to note that Dante was an Italian who lived about the time of Boniface VIII. He started writing his famous 'Divina Comedia' in 1300.

There are other medieval elements in this gospel. To mention just a few, in chapter 194, for example it is said that the family of Lazarus were overlords of two towns, Magdala and Bethany. Roman forces controlled most of the lands of Palestine in those days, so no such system of overlord rule was known. This is the kind of feudal rule which became common in the Middle Ages.

The reference to wine casks in chapter 152 is an obvious anachronism. The court procedures described in chapter

121 demand that the author would have had to be familiar with a medieval society. In the light of the preceding and many other evidences, both external and internal, it can be seen that this gospel must have been written by someone living many centuries after the Barnabas of the New Testament.

Particular errors and contradictions are listed here:

1. This gospel states that Jesus was born while Pilate was a governor in Palestine. According to history, however, Pilate did not become a governor until 26 CE. Also, in chapter 3, the birth of Jesus is placed during the time of the high priesthood of Annas (6–15 CE) and Caiaphas (18–36 CE), which contradicts not only history but the gospel itself. Neither of them was in power when Jesus was born. The Barnabas gospel is wrong by about ten years with Annas, by twenty-two years with Caiaphas and by thirty years with Pilate.

2. Herod (Antipas) is mentioned as having power and many soldiers at his command in Jerusalem and Judea (Barnabas, chapter 214). This is a blunder because he ruled only in Galilee some sixty miles away. This gospel calls him a Gentile (Barnabas, chapter 217), although he was a practising Jew. He was only in Jerusalem to celebrate the feast of the Passover, which is why he was able to be consulted during Jesus' trial.

3. In chapter 80 it is stated that Daniel was only two years old when he was captured by Nebuchadnezzar. This conflicts with the account in the Bible (Daniel chapter 2), which says that Nebuchadnezzar consulted Daniel in the second year of his reign concerning his dream. He was so impressed by Daniel's wisdom that he appointed

him a ruler over the province of Babylon. If the testimony of this gospel is accepted then Daniel would have to be three years old at this point.

4. Chapter 91 relates the account of the amassing of three armies, each of 200,000 armed men in a battle over the question of Christ's deity. Under Roman rule at that time both the possession of arms and the manufacture of arms were strictly controlled. Also, according to Encyclopaedia Britannica, the whole Roman regular army only numbered 300,000 at this time and half of these were reserves. There was only a small garrison in Judea until the Roman destruction of Jerusalem in 68–70 CE.[15]

5. In chapter 127 of this gospel, Jesus is mentioned as preaching from the pinnacle of the Temple. This was hardly a suitable place from which to preach as it was about two hundred metres above the ground and so he would not have been heard. The author displays here an ignorance of a very basic part of his life – if indeed he was the Barnabas of the New Testament.

6. Nazareth is described as a coastal city on the sea of Galilee, in chapters 20 and 21. This town still exists but is thirteen hundred feet above sea level and twenty kilometres from the sea. In chapter 99 Tiro (Tyre/Tyrus) is presented as being close to the Jordan, which is not correct. Tyrus is fifty kilometres away on the shore of the Mediterranean sea in present day Lebanon. If the writer walked these areas with Jesus, why does he confuse such facts? Zacchaeus is said to have encountered Jesus in Nazareth, while the gospel according to Luke says this happened in or near Jericho (Luke 19).

---

[15] *The New Encyclopaedia Britannica*, Vol. 25, pp. 414–415 (Ed. 15th, 1993).

7. Chapter 169 of this gospel portrays a European summer. This contrasts with the Palestinian summer where rain falls in winter and fields are parched in summer, anything but green as mentioned in the text. According to the context, Jesus was in the wilderness of Jordan where he certainly would not be enjoying beautiful European-type summer scenery.

8. Haggai and Hosea are two separate prophets whose revelations are separately recorded in two books in the Old Testament but this gospel says that their story is related in the book of Daniel (Barnabas, chapter 185). His confusion concerning Bible references is further demonstrated in chapters 165 and 169 where he mixes quotations together.

9. The writer claims that Jesus is not the Messiah and yet uses the messianic title 'Son of David' for him (Barnabas chapters 11, 19, 21 and so on). In chapter 19 the primacy of Jesus is taught but refuted in chapters 54 and 55, where Muhammad is stated as having the primacy at the last judgement.

The Gospel of Barnabas in conflict with Islam

The Qur'an expects a Muslim to believe in the books of God which he gave to Moses, David, Jesus and other prophets. According to Islamic teachings, these books should in no way contradict each other. Muslims believe that if the Bible differs it must be because it has been corrupted. Many Muslims think that the Gospel of Barnabas is in harmony with the Qur'an in its teaching about the crucifixion and other matters. Therefore, they claim, it must be the one and only true Gospel, the original.

Here are a few important points about which the Qur'an and this gospel are not in harmony:

1. According to some Muslims' understanding, the original Gospel descended upon Jesus. While the Gospel of Barnabas does indeed claim that it descended into the heart of Jesus (Barnabas, chapter 10), it does not specify that Jesus received God's words precisely from a heavenly copy of the book. The writer does not appear to subscribe to this Muslim view of inspiration.

2. Christ is spoken of as having voiced and believed the Muslim creed *Shahada*, 'There is no God but Allah and Muhammad is his prophet'. This creed was not laid down until 600 years after Jesus. Even in the Qur'an it is never given as one complete statement at one time.

3. This gospel presents Jesus and his mission as being identical to that of John the Baptist in the role of forerunner to the Messiah, who is Muhammad (Barnabas, chapters 42–44 and 220). It completely omits John the Baptist and his ministry, whilst both the Qur'an and the New Testament acknowledge his prophethood and teach that he was a forerunner of Jesus. Moreover, the Qur'an accepts Jesus as the Messiah but the Jesus in this gospel refuses to accept the title. In several passages this gospel openly suggests that Jesus is not the Messiah (Barnabas, chapters 42, 82, 83, 96, 97, 198, 206).

4. This gospel portrays Mary as giving birth to Jesus without pain (Barnabas, chapter 3) and that his birth took place in a shepherd's house or shelter. However, the Qur'an relates the pangs of childbirth, which drove Mary to cry out in pain and that

Jesus was born under a palm tree in the wilderness.

5. Many Muslims believe that Allah has sent 124,000 prophets into the world, but this gospel places the count at 144,000 (Barnabas, chapter 17).

6. It tells us that God sent a group of believers to hell for 70,000 years (Barnabas, chapter 137), whereas the Qur'an says that God would not harm a believer even so much as by the weight of an ant (Surah 4:40).

7. According to the teaching of this gospel when the *Tawrat* became contaminated, God sent another book, the *Zabur* or Psalms. When this was altered by people, God gave the *Injil* – the Gospel to replace it. This theory holds that when a divine book is altered or corrupted, God sends another book. Consequently, when the Gospel was corrupted God sent the Qur'an. This raises an important question with regard to the Gospel of Barnabas. If, as many Muslims believe, this is an unaltered version of the true and original Gospel, then there was no need to send the Qur'an to replace it.

8. According to this gospel, there are nine heavens and ten hells (Barnabas, chapters 52, 57, 178), however, the Qur'an teaches only seven heavens (Surah 2:29).

9. This gospel teaches that Satan is the creator of hell (Barnabas, chapter 35), whereas the Qur'an teaches that God is Creator of hell (Surah 25:11).

10. In this gospel, it is stated that before the last day there will be a fifteen-day schedule of step-by-step destruction (Barnabas, chapter 53). It further states that on the thirteenth day the heavens shall be rolled up like a book and every living

thing shall die. All this is in clear contradiction
of the Qur'an which states that men will be alive
until the last day (Surah 80:33–37). The Qur'an
nowhere mentions the death of the holy angels,
but asserts that they will still perform their duty
(Surah 69:15–17).

11. Jesus is alleged to have said that a man should content himself with one wife, whereas the Qur'an
permits up to four wives (Surah 4:3; Barnabas,
chapter 115).

12. In chapters 32, 66 and 67 of this gospel Jesus is
made to say that offerings and sacrifices are not
part of God's command but are man-made traditions. In other words this gospel denies that God
ordered burnt sacrifices in the Torah. However the
Qur'an confirms that God did order the Israelites
to offer sacrifices (Qur'an, Surah 2:67–72; Bible,
Numbers 19:1–10).

It is obvious that although these two documents, and the
people who support them, share the same theology concerning the crucifixion of Jesus, there is very little else
upon which their teachings coincide.

Ahmadiyya in Islam and this gospel

In India around the year 1879 a Muslim, Mirza Ghulam
Ahmad (1835–1908), came to believe that he had been chosen by God as a reformer of Islam. He established his own
movement, *Ahmadiyyat*, and very soon promulgated
many changes to the beliefs of orthodox Muslims. He
believed that he himself was the *Mahdi* – the reviver of
Islam and the second coming of Jesus in the Spirit. Orthodox Muslims were incensed but could not stop him.

Today according to Ahmadiyya sources there are about twelve million adherents of this sect in the world.

Ahmad, influenced perhaps by Western philosophies, announced a new doctrine, foreign to Islam, that Jesus had indeed been crucified. He went on to claim that Jesus was rescued from the cross in a state of collapse, recovered in secret, and after passing through India he reached Kashmir, where he died at the age of one hundred and twenty. Ahmad argued vociferously against orthodox Muslims, saying: 'Those Muslims who believe Jesus to be in heaven in his physical body, are guilty of uttering an absurdity against the Qur'an.' It is surprising, however, to find that Ahmad and his followers support this gospel of Barnabas. He wrote, 'the gospel of Barnabas, which contains the prophecy about the latter day prophet, is declared by Christians to be forged, because it contains a clear prophecy about the Holy prophet.' He gives two reasons why Christians reject this gospel: 'that the book or the story happens to contradict the Gospels in use;' and 'that the book or the story happens to agree with the Holy Qur'an.'[16] To what extent the gospel of Barnabas is in conflict with the Qur'an, has already been shown. So, how does this gospel compare with the Ahmadiyya sect?

1. The Ahmadiyya movement believes that their leader was a prophet of God after Muhammad. In contrast this gospel states that 'there shall not come after him true prophets sent by God, but there shall come a great number of false prophets …' (Barnabas, chapter 97).

2. The gospel of Barnabas relates the stories of the healing of the sick and the raising of the dead by Jesus. The Ahmadiyya movement does not believe in these miracles. Mirza Ahmad wrote in one of his

---

[16] Ghulam Ahmad, *Chashma Masihi*, p.6.

books, '... a thing which is not possible for the Holy prophet (Muhammad) – the best of prophets ... how can it be so for the Messiah (Jesus)!'[17]

3. This gospel denies Jesus the title of Messiah and yet the Ahmadiyya accept it as a fact, as seen from the above quote.

4. Mirza Ahmad is very suspicious about the authenticity of the four gospel accounts in the New Testament. He says that these gospels contain many things which show that they have not been preserved in their original form. For example, he refers to Luke 7:36–50 and comments that no prophet 'had ever set such an example of freedom that he would allow an impure and adulterous woman, a noted sinner, to touch his body with her hands, to let her rub oil into his head – bought out of her immoral gains – and to rub her hair on his feet.'[18] On this he bases his conclusion that the four Gospels are not in their authentic form. Yet the very same story is recounted in the gospel of Barnabas (Barnabas, chapters 129–130).

5. Mirza Ahmad believes that just as John the Baptist was Elijah in the spirit, (Matthew 11:14; 17:12), so he himself is Jesus in the spirit. Where does he get his knowledge of John the Baptist being Elijah in the Spirit? Certainly not from the Qur'an because it does not mention him being Elijah and certainly not from the 'one true gospel' – the gospel of Barnabas where the Baptist is never once mentioned. He took it from the Bible (Malachi 4), which he says he does not believe.

6. This gospel of Barnabas says that Judas was crucified in the place of Jesus, while the Ahmadiyya

---

[17] Ghulam Ahmad, *Tawzih Maram*, (English tr.) pp.6–7.
[18] Ghulam Ahmad, *Jesus in India*, p.47.

movement believe that it was really Jesus. Further, this gospel would have us believe that Jesus was taken into heaven bodily before the crucifixion, while the Ahmadiyya believe that he was crucified but did not die on the cross. They say, '. . . it is impossible for us to think that Jesus the Messiah is alive in heaven while Muhammad, our Holy prophet lies buried in the earth. We cannot think so . . .'[19] So, as in the case of the orthodox Muslims, the Ahmadiyya movement is in a very precarious position, if they depend on this gospel to confirm Mirza Ahmad's teachings.

Conclusion

This gospel of Barnabas is a prime example of what happens when a spurious work is subjected to critical review. When all the errors and inconsistencies are considered, this gospel is exposed as a product of a 'Pseudo-Barnabas' who was never a first-century disciple of Jesus nor had ever been in the land where Jesus walked and taught.

---

[19] Bashiruddin, *Invitation to Ahmadiyyat*, p.15.

8

The inimitability of the Scriptures

The majority of Muslims affirm their faith in the miraculous nature of the Qur'an, *Ijaz al-Qur'an*. They claim that the Qur'anic text is *Lathani*, unique in Arabic literature, and because of its divine origin, no text 'like' it can be produced. To support this belief, Muhammad is reported as saying, 'Every prophet was given miracles because of which people believed, but what I have been given is divine inspiration which Allah has revealed to me.'[1] While holding to this doctrine, Muslims reject the Bible because they feel its teaching and content is not eloquent nor is it unique in style in the same way as the text of the Qur'an is. Furthermore, the Bible is said to be unreliable because it is not unique.

In this chapter, we will survey the background of this popular doctrine and the context of verses of the Qur'an that are used to support it. We will consider some probing questions. In the light of Islamic history, is there any validity in this claim that no one is able to respond to the challenge of the Qur'an? When the Qur'an issues a challenge to produce a work similar to itself, does it intend the challenge to refer to the chance to equal or excel the Qur'an in terms of its status in being *hiddaya* (guidance), *balagha*, (rhetoric) or even *fasaha* (eloquence)?

---

[1] *Sahih al-Bukhari*, Vol. 6, p.474.

The challenge of the Qur'an

When Muhammad preached to the Makkan polytheists, they did not welcome the message. They accused Muhammad of inventing the contents of the Qur'an, and said that it merely contained old fables. In response Muhammad issued a challenge to his detractors to produce anything like it. This challenge (*tahaddi*) is repeated in several verses (both Makkan and Madinan) with varying degrees of emphasis:

> If you are in doubt as to what We have revealed from time to time to Our Servant, then produce a Surah like thereunto . . . (Surah 2:23–4)

> Say: 'Then bring ye a Book from Allah, which is a better Guide than either of them, that I may follow it! (Do), if ye are truthful!' (Surah 28:49)

> Or they may say, 'He forged it.' Say, 'Bring ye then ten Surahs forged, like unto it, and call (to your aid) whomsoever ye can, other than Allah! – if ye speak the truth!' (Surah 11:13)

> This Qur'an is not such as can be produced by other than Allah; on the contrary it is a confirmation of (revelations) that went before it, and a fuller explanation of the Book – wherein there is no doubt – from the Lord of the World. Or do they say, 'He forged it'? Say: 'Bring then a Surah like unto it, and call (to your aid) anyone you can beside Allah, if it be ye speak the truth!' (Surah 10:37–38)

> Say if the whole of mankind and Jinns were to gather together to produce the like of this Qur'an they could not produce the like thereof, even if they backed up each other with help and support. (Surah 17:88)

Or do they say, 'He fabricated (the Message)'? Nay, they have
no faith! Let them then produce a recital like unto it – if (it be)
they speak the Truth! (Surah 52:33–34)

Many Muslims claim that, 'This challenge posed by the
Qur'an has never been met.'[2] Such a claim compels us to
examine carefully the background of the revelation of
these passages, their causes, and to look into the relevant
period of Islamic history.

Contextual background

In two of these five passages, the challenge is identical,
while in the remaining three there are separate and different demands being made. These demands range from a
whole Qur'an to a single piece. The difference between the
forms of Muhammad's challenges have caused some
scholars to explain away this inconsistency by saying that
the challenges were made at different times. At first, disbelievers were called upon to produce the like of the
whole of the Qur'an. When they failed to do so, the challenge was whittled down to the production of the like of
ten chapters. When, however, they were unable to produce even ten chapters, the challenge was further reduced
to the production of a single chapter; and lastly the disbelievers were challenged to produce even a single passage
like any passage of the Qur'an.

Such an explanation does not seem to hold water
because when we study the *Asbabun Nuzul* (the reason
and the time of revelation), the order of these passages is
as follows: Surah 52; Surah 17; Surah 11; Surah 28; Surah
10 and Surah 2.[3] Now in Surah 52, the first to be revealed in

---

[2] Ahmad von Denffer, *Ulum al-Qur'an*, p.151.
[3] Sell, *The Historical Development of the Qur'an*, pp.vii–viii. For
detailed chronology of the Qur'an see Watt & Bell, *Introduction
to the Qur'an*, pp.108–120.

the order, the challenge is not qualified by any condition as regards to the size. The opponents have been given the choice of simply producing a single passage. It is very strange that whereas at first the challenge was unqualified and the opposition was called upon to produce even a short passage, later it began to be made harder and hedged round by conditions and stipulations.

Makkan passages

It was in Makkah that Muhammad is said to have presented the first passages of the Qur'an to the people. Interestingly the reaction of the people is also narrated in different parts of the Qur'an. When the Makkans heard about his claim to prophethood, they ignored him and made a joke of it. Later, they accused him of plagiarism by declaring that the contents of his revelation were 'Fables of the men of old which he hath written down . . .' (Surah 25:5). During the first thirteen years of his mission in Makkah, Muhammad's complaint was, 'my own folk make this Qur'an of no account' (Surah 25:30). Early Muslim historians and *traditionists* report many incidents from this era, about Muhammad's call, his invitations and his suffering, but, remarkably, there is no mention of these challenges in the present form to be found in today's Qur'an.

In those days at the annual fair of Ukaz, authors, rhetoricians, poets and story tellers gathered to compete with each other. It was also the custom of the time for poets and orators to hang up their compositions upon the Ka'ba's walls. However, within the information available about such activities, there is no record of Muhammad calling for *tahaddi*, a challenge. Rather, he is found in seclusion. Those who wanted to meet him encountered many barriers. For example Ibn Abbas relates Abu Dhar's longing to see Muhammad and how Ali helps him in a very artful way, '. . . if I see any danger for you I will stop as if to pass water, but if I go on, follow me and enter the place which I will enter.'[4] Further, one may learn through Abdullah bin Samat that it was only at night, when people were asleep, that Muhammad used to go to the Ka'ba to walk round it in the usual ritual and to offer prayer.[5] He did not recite the Qur'an aloud. And to diminish the risk of being over-heard he told his followers, *'La tajher besalateka'* – 'Be not loud voiced in thy prayer' (Surah 17:110).[6]

According to Muslim scholars, Surah 10 *(Yunus)*, Surah 11 *(Hud)*, and Surah 52 *(Al-Tur)* were revealed to Muhammad in Makkah. Critics believe that since Muslims were advised to keep quiet and not to perform their prayers or recite the Qur'an openly, it is most unlikely that the challenge given in these Surahs would be heard by everyone openly by his opponents during the Makkan period of Muhammad's mission. They do not constitute an *open* challenge.

Madinan passages

Now three references remain. Although commentators believe that Surah 17 *(al-Isra)* was also revealed in Makkah, some state that the *tahaddi* (challenge) verse was revealed in Madina while to others it is purely a matter of conjecture.[7] Surah 28 *(al-Qasas)* is also a late Makkan Surah. Others say it was revealed to Muhammad when fleeing from Mecca on his way to Madina.[8]

The context of the passage in this Surah suggests that Muhammad gave equal status to the Torah and the

---

4   *Sahih al-Bukhari*, Vol. 5, p.127.
5   *Sahih al-Muslim*, Vol. 4, pp.1316–1319.
6   *Sahih al-Bukhari*, Vol. 6, p.208.
7   Muhammad Asad, *The Message of the Qur'an*, p.417.
8   Pickthall, *Holy Qur'an*, p.380.

Qur'an. In his challenge he asked, '. . . bring a Scripture from the presence of Allah that giveth clearer guidance than these two (that) I may follow it . . .' (Surah 28:49). The context of the passage suggest that the word *two* in this verse refers to the Torah and the Qur'an. This means that the Torah has an equal standing with the Qur'an in terms of its teaching and guidance. Such a statement in the Qur'an thus undermines the claim that the Qur'an is unique, *Lathani*. Further the passage reveals that the challenge was not to match style or diction or in other words *balagha* (rhetoric) or *fasaha* (eloquence) but in terms of its being *hiddaya* (guidance).

Concerning the 'challenge verse' in Surah 2 *(al-Baqarah)*, some prominent members of the Shia sect of Islam believe that this verse has suffered alteration. Imam Jafar Sadiq (d.765) said that this verse was revealed regarding Ali ibn Abi Talib (d.661) and the verse originally was: 'If you are in doubt as to what We have revealed from time to time to Our Servant regarding Ali, then produce a Surah like thereunto …'.[9]

Critics assert that one has to look at the time and circumstances of revelation to gain a complete understanding of a passage in the Qur'an. This Surah was revealed during the first four years after the Hijra. It was a time when the *umah*, Muslim community, under the leadership of Muhammed, had gained control in and around Madinah, and was well placed to overcome the opposition in Makkah. Those who wanted to respond to the Surah and its challenge would therefore have been very careful. Still, there is some historical evidence that several opponents did respond to the challenge (see below).

---

[9] Ahmad Abdullah Salamah, *The Sunni and Shia Perspective of the Holy Qur'an*, p.15.

Style and diction: a proof of inspiration

It is important to note that nowhere in the Qur'an itself is there a claim for it to be a unique example of Arabic literature. It is also arguable whether excellence in eloquence and rhetoric is proof of a work being a miracle, or that the author or compiler should be treated as a prophet. If it were so, the world would have accepted several authors who could compare with the prophet of Islam. Homer for example was not only illiterate but also blind, yet he was the author of the Iliad and much of the Odyssey. He was the greatest Greek epic poet in terms of eloquence, versification and style. However, it does not prove that his work has a divine origin. Similarly, there is pre-Islamic poetry in Arabic of very high quality that is still available to us, but no one believes that those works were divinely inspired. To discredit the Bible in this way despite its known literary qualities and to believe in the Qur'an because of certain literary characteristics, is not a balanced judgement.

The difference between the Qur'an and non-Qur'anic texts

Although Muslims claim that no one has ever produced a text like the Qur'an, the opposite is true. Islamic history itself contains evidence that people were capable of writing something like the text of the Qur'an. For example, at the time when the Qur'an was compiled into one volume, the traditions state that people used to come to Zaid Bin Thabit with verses of the Qur'an but he would not add them to the Qur'an unless a trustworthy witness backed it up.[10] If the text of the Qur'an had been so unique,

---

[10] Suyuti, *Al-Itqan fi Ulum al-Qur'an*, Vol 1, p.157.

obviously there would have been no need for witnesses; the text would have been self-authenticating. In fact we learn that there was quite a disagreement between the Companions of Muhammad about several parts of the Qur'an.

Ibn Masood, a prominent companion of the Prophet, as mentioned elsewhere, did not accept the first and the last two surahs as being part of the Qur'an. So if the Qur'an had been unique in terms of its inimitability, Ibn Masood would not have had such reservations. On the other hand Ubay b. Ka'b included two extra surahs namely *Al-Hafd* (the haste) and *Al-Khal* (the separation). A version of these verses, though not part of the present Qur'an, is still recited in the late evening prayer, *Isha*.[11] Further, if it was beyond human power to equal the Qur'anic verses, then some of the sects would not have had doubts about some parts of the Qur'an, as did the Memoniah sect which refused to accept the Surah *Yusuf* as part of the Qur'an.[12]

Arabic language

In the light of Surah 16:103 and 41:44, some people believe that the Qur'an is inimitable because it is in pure Arabic and its language is not mixed with any foreign words. This view is mistaken because the Qur'an *does* contain foreign vocabulary. In his book, *Itqan fi Ulum al-Qur'an*, Suyuti lists about 118 non-Arabic words recorded in the Qur'an.[13] Certainly it can be argued that a few non-Arabic words do not make the Qur'an non-Arabic. However the question is not whether or not the Qur'an is in Arabic but whether the Qur'an contains or does not contain words that are of non-Arabic origin. Critics say that since the

[11] Suyuti, *Al-Itqan fi Ulum al-Qur'an*, Vol 1, pp.172 and 175.
[12] Imam Zahra, *Islami Mazahib* (tr. Urdu), p.133.
[13] Suyuti, *Al-Itqan fi Ulum al-Qur'an*, Vol 2, pp.105–106.

Qur'an denies that it has non-Arabic words, there is an internal contradiction.

Generally, it is believed and taught that the Qur'an is the best example of all linguistic and grammatical composition, structure and other rules of Arabic. However, careful readers find passages that are inconsistent and are not in compliance with usual Arabic grammar. Even some Muslim scholars admit there are grammatical irregularities in the Qur'an. For example in Surah 2:177 *wa assabireena* should be *assabiruna*. In Surah 2:124 the word *az-zalimina* should be *az-zalimuna*. In Surah 5:69 *Sabi'una* should be *sabi'ina*. In Surah 7:56 the word *qaribun* should be *qaribatun*. In Surah 7:160 *ithnatay ashrata asbatan* should be *ithnay ashra sibtan*. In Surah 20:63 the Arabic *hazani* should be *hazaini*. Other examples occur in Surah 3:39; 4:162; 7:16; 21:3; 22:19; 49:9 and 63:10.

The Qur'an also has incomplete sentences, and phrases which have been omitted. This obscures the meaning. Ali Dashti writes that the Qur'an 'contains sentences which are incomplete and not fully intelligible without the aid of the commentaries; foreign words, unfamiliar Arabic words, and words used with other than the normal meaning; adjectives and verbs inflected without observance of the concords of gender and number; illogically and ungrammatically applied pronouns which sometimes have no referent; and (in rhymed passages) predicates which are often remote from the subjects.'[14]

Suyuti, in his *Itqan*, discusses this matter and points out many *makhzoof*, omitted words and sentences. He has devoted several pages to giving examples. For example, he quotes Surah 22:32 'Thus should come from the piety of heart' and says that it should be understood as 'Thus its

---

[14] Dashti, *Twenty Three Years*, p.48.

glorification comes from the deeds of those of piety of heart.'[15]

Another example is from Surah 20:96, which says, 'So I took a handful (of dust) from the foot print of the Messenger.' According to Suyuti it should be understood as: 'So I took a handful (of dust) from the footprint of the hoof of the Messenger's mare.'[16]

In Surah 12, the end of verse 45 and the beginning of 46 suggest that obviously some narrative is missing between 'Send ye me' and 'O Joseph . . .'. To solve this abrupt jump from one scene to another Suyuti says it should read, 'Send ye me to Joseph to ask him for the interpretation of the dream. So he did. He came to him and said, "O Joseph . . ."'[17]

Inimitability in accurate information and teaching

Beliefs about the Qur'an are also based on the claim that, in contrast to the Bible, it contains accurate information about the past and future and that it is free from any discrepancies. Some writers try to demonstrate how the Qur'an is scientifically accurate. Their aim is to show the miraculous character of the Qur'an in predicting scientific discoveries which are known now but have only recently been 'proved'.[18] However, one could argue that neither the Qur'an, nor the Bible, nor any other religious book

---

[15] Suyuti, *Al-Itqan fi Ulum al-Qur'an*, Vol 2, p.159.

[16] Suyuti, *Al-Itqan fi Ulum al-Qur'an*, Vol 2, p.159.

[17] Suyuti, *Al-Itqan fi Ulum al-Qur'an*, Vol 2, p.160.

[18] See for example: 1. Afzalur Rahman, *Qur'anic Sciences*, (The Muslim Schools Trust, London 1981); 2. Ahmad Mahmud Soliaman, *Scientific trends in the Qur'an*, (Taha Publishers, London, 1985); 3. Maurice Bucaille, *The Bible, the Qur'an and Science*, (Indianapolis: American Trust Publication, 1978).

contains many scientific facts which could not have been obtained by human observation, except possibly the story of creation.

There are certainly verses in the Qur'an which could be used to demonstrate the scientific insight of the Qur'an. The same 'demonstration' of insight has also been done in the case of the Bible. There are however other verses in the Qur'an that conflict with the available scientific information. For example the Qur'an claims that the sun sets in a muddy spring of water (Surah 18:86) and that coral is extracted from a river (Surah 55:22). Similarly, a Hadith says that the sun goes under the throne of God.[19]

Another view is that the Qur'an is a miracle because of its unique teaching. However, we find that the laws and ordinances which the Qur'an contains are, in fact, too brief and insufficient for the needs of the Muslim *Umah*. There are only some 200 verses that deal with Islamic *Shariah*. Even with the traditions and the *Sunnah*, these sources were not enough; further interpretation and exposition was needed. Thus the development of Islamic jurisprudence was undertaken, which only became a reasonably complete system after several centuries of work by Muslim scholars.

Many of the principles mentioned among the brief laws and ordinances of the Qur'an were in fact conceived first many centuries before Muhammad. Teachers like Confucius, Buddha, Zoroaster, Socrates, Moses and Jesus said similar things long before Muhammad. The articles of Islamic faith and the 'five pillars of Islam' were common practice among people before Muhammad. Whether it be prayer, fasting, *Hajj*, *Jihad* or *Zakah*, the teaching was already available. Also, the majority of the stories of the Qur'an, the narrative of the creation, the flood, Abraham

---

[19] *Sahih al-Bukhari*, Vol. 6, p.154.

and the offering of his son, the histories of Lot, Joseph, Moses and Pharaoh etc., (some of which are repeated over and over), were already available in the Bible. The Qur'an itself claims to be in the revealed books of the former people (Surah 26:196). Furthermore, it claims to have been given lest the Arabs make excuses that they cannot understand the languages in which the earlier books were revealed (Surah 6:157,158).

Belief by conviction or fear

Popular belief is that the Arabs became Muslims because they had no answer to the challenge of the Qur'an. However, in every case where Islamic history can be quoted in support of such a view, other historical examples can be quoted to contradict it.

1. *A report in favour*

Alqama bin Abdul Manaf is mentioned as having testified about the miracle of the Qur'an when he addressed the leaders of the Quraish. He said, 'Oh Quraish, a new calamity has befallen you. Muhammad was a young man the most liked among you, most truthful in speech, and most trustworthy, until, when you saw grey hairs on his temple, and he brought you his message, you said that he was a sorcerer, but he is not, for we have seen such people and their spitting and their knots; you said, a diviner, but we have seen such people and their behaviour, and we have heard their rhymes; you said a soothsayer, but he is not a soothsayer, for we have heard their rhymes; and you said a poet, but he is not a poet, for we have heard all kinds of poetry; you said he was possessed, but he is not for we have seen the possessed and he shows no signs of their gasping and whispering and delirium. Oh men of

Quraish, look to your affairs, for by Allah a serious thing has befallen you.'[20]

Professor Abdel Haleem quotes one of Muhammad's opponents, saying that he 'was in awe of the power of the Qur'an's language describing it by saying, "It ascends to the heights, and nothing ascends above it, and it crushes what is beneath it." '[21]

2. A report in opposition

There are many reports in apparent contradiction of such claims of perfection which suggest that it was not because of the unique message and its style that most people became Muslims. For example, Usama bin Zaid reports that once he went with Muhammad to visit a sick friend, Sa'd bin Ubada. On the way to him, they passed beside a gathering in which Abdullah bin Ubai was sitting with a group including Muslims and some pagan idolaters and Jews. Muhammad paused and recited to them some verses of his revelation. Ubai became angry and said to Muhammad, 'O man! There is nothing better than what you say, if it is the truth. So do not trouble us with it in our gatherings, but if somebody comes to you, you can preach to him.' The fight that was about to begin between the rival groups was apparently averted.

Note, however that the same Usama is related elsewhere as having said, 'When Allah's Apostle had fought the battle of Badr and Allah killed many among the chiefs of the infidels and the nobles of the Quraish, and Allah's apostle and his companions had returned with victory and booty . . . Abdullah bin Ubai . . . and the pagan idolaters who were with him, said, "This matter (Islam) has now brought out its face (triumphed), so give Allah's

---

[20] http://www.ummah.org.uk/islamaware/Quss.html.
[21] Haleem, *Understanding the Qur'an: Themes and Style*, p.8.

Apostle the pledge of allegiance . . . Then they became Muslims" '.[22]

3. The influx of believers

In the passage immediately above, we see one answer to the puzzle: the prophet's followers did become Muslims not because the Qur'an was such an eloquent miracle, but for fear of being left unprotected away from the 'umbrella' of Muhammad and his followers. The number of Muslims started to grow very quickly after the victory over Makkah. On the day of the conquest of Makkah, Muhammad is said to have been reciting the Qur'an 'in a vibrating and pleasant voice.'[23] In the very place where he had advised his followers not to raise their voice in worship, he now said that whoever did not recite the Qur'an aloud was not among his followers.[24]

According to Ibn Ishaq, the Quraish became subject to Muhammad when Makkah was occupied, and he subdued it to Islam. Other Arabs knew that it was dangerous to fight the apostle, or to display enmity towards him; thus, as Ishaq puts it, they entered into God's religion *in batches* from all directions.[25] One can choose to believe that the superiority of the Qur'an was demonstrated because the opposition could not produce the like of it, whereas in fact it is more likely that they feared *military* elimination if they opposed Muhammad.

Meeting the challenge

In spite of the above criticisms, Muslims religiously believe the Qur'an has an incomparable and inimitable

---

[22] *Sahih al-Bukhari*, Vol. 8, pp.145–147.

[23] *Sahih al-Bukhari*, Vol. 9, p.474.

[24] *Sahih al-Bukhari*, Vol. 9, pp.464, 476–477.

[25] Ibn Hisham, *Sirat Rasul Allah*, (tr. Guillaume, E)., *The Life of Muhammad*, p.685.

quality in terms of its literary style and message. They continue to claim that the 'challenge posed by the Qur'an has never been met'.[26] They do so because the Qur'an claims that its text 'is not such as can be produced by other than Allah' (Surah 10:37; 17:88). Their argument is that God is omnipotent and omniscient and when he says in the Qur'an, *Wa lan tafalu*, 'and of a surety you cannot', he means what he says. Thus, no one has and no one can imitate the Qur'an.

Such a stance cannot be taken lightly. The assertion that nobody in the world has or could have produced a small chapter just like the Qur'an not only contradicts the facts but also challenges the veracity of many Muslim historians. The fact is that some did take up the challenge and did produce texts like the Qur'an, although Muslims did not acknowledge their worth. Their material was destroyed, and they themselves were killed to ensure the fulfilment of the claim that the 'Qur'an both predicts and asserts that no one can bring forth its like either in form or meaning'.[27]

Issa Boulata comments that 'There are a few attempts recorded in the Islamic tradition. What remains of their texts, understandably suppressed by orthodoxy, are snippets of ludicrous parodies that have a hollow ring to them and that do no credit to their authors.'[28] Rudi Paret believes that the challenge was a 'rhetorical device' and should not be taken seriously. He says that this belief is taught so that the Qur'an is shielded from study by literary historians – a stance which has had a serious effect on Islam to this day.[29]

---

[26] Ahmad von Denffer, *Ulum al-Qur'an*, p.151.
[27] Fadhlalla Haeri, *Man in Qur'an and the Meaning of the Furqan*, p.22.
[28] Rippin, *Approaches to the History of the Interpretation of the Qur'an*, p.141.
[29] Beeston, *Arabic Literature to the End of the Umayyad Period*, p.215.

Imraul Qais' daughter's question

Imraul Qais (d.540) was one of the most expressive of Arab poets. Some of his poems were among the most famous *Muallaqat*, that is, poems displayed on the Ka'ba in Makkah before Islam. Four verses from one of his poems also appear in the Qur'an (Surah 54:1,29,31,46). It is said that when Imraul Qais' granddaughter heard the Surah recited aloud, she immediately recognised the poem and demanded to know how those verses had become part of Muhammad's revelation. Qadhi Imam Abdullah al-Hussain in his *Sharah Muallaqat* quotes from Imraul Qais. A passage is illustrated as it appears in al-Hussain's book. Verses marked with a line above them occur also in

Figure 16. Some verses of Imraul Qais

Some verses of the Arab poet Qais. Words marked with a line above occur also in the Qur'an with very slight differences.

the Qur'an, with very slight differences but the meaning remains the same.[30]

Nadr Ibn Harith

We learn from Ibn Ishaq (d.707) through Ibn Hisham (d.830) in his *Sira* (Life of Muhammad) and other reliable sources that Nadr ibn Harith (d.624) 'had been to al-Hira and learnt there the tales of the Kings of Persia, the tales of Rustum and Isbandyar.' He had produced these tales in a style similar to the Qur'an and read them out at meetings. Whenever Muhammad held meetings, Nadr used to come in and get up 'when the prophet sat down' and used to say, 'I can tell a better story than he.'[31] He would challenge Muhammad and say, 'In what respect is Muhammad a better storyteller than I?', adding, 'By God, Muhammad cannot tell a better story than I and his talk is only old fables which he has copied as I have.'[32]

According to Ibn Abbas and others, Muhammad received several Qur'anic verses from God in reference to Nadr at various times, e.g. Surah 68:15;[33] Surah 83:13; Surah 45:7; Surah 21:26–30,98,101.[34] Some Muslims believe that a passage in the late Makkan Surahs was also concerning people like Nadr: 'But there are among men, those who purchase idle tales, without knowledge (or meaning), to mislead (men) from the Path of Allah and throw ridicule (on the Path): for such there will be a humiliating penalty' (Surah 31:5).[35]

---

[30] Abu Abdullah al-Hussain, *Sharah Mu'allaqat*, Matbua Iran, cited by Tisdall in his, *Yanabiul Islam*, (Urdu), p.19–21.

[31] Ibn Hisham, *Sira* (tr. A. Guillaume), p.136.

[32] Ibn Hisham, *Sira*, p.162.

[33] Ibid, p.136.

[34] Ibid, p.162.

[35] Edward Sell, *The Historical Development of the Qur'an*, p.52.

At the Battle of Badr, Nadr was taken prisoner by the Muslims. His relatives offered a ransom for him, but they were refused and Nadr was put to death.[36] Ibn Hisham has recorded a lamentation by Qutayla d. Al-Harith, sister of al-Nadr.[37]

Musaylima b. Habib al-Hanafi

There were some like *Musaylima b. Habib al-Hanafi*, *al-Aswad b. Ka'b al-Ansi* and *Tulayha b. Khuwaylid al-Asadi* who claimed to be prophets like Muhammad. *Musaylima* claimed that he had received a Qur'an from God, the *Ar-Rahman*. About 100,000 are said to have followed him. It was in the reign of Abu Bakr that Muslims fought a battle with them in 633 at a place called Aqraba in Al-Yamama.[38] Musaylima and most of his followers

---

[36] Ibn Hisham, *Sirah*, p.308.

[37] Ibn Hisham, *Sirah*, p.360. The following is the English translation:

O Rider, I think you will reach Uthayl
At dawn of the fifth night if you are lucky.
Greet a dead man there for me.
Swift camels always carry news from me to thee.
(Tell of) flowing tears running profusely or ending in a sob.
Can al-Nadr hear me when I call him,
How can a dead man hear who cannot speak?
O Muhammad, finest child of noble mother,
Whose sire a noble sire was,
'Twould not have harmed you had you spared him.
(A warrior oft spares though full of rage and anger.)
Or you could have taken a ransom,
The dearest price that could be paid.
Al-Nadr was the nearest relative you captured
With the best claim to be released.
The swords of his father's sons came down on him.
Good God, what bonds of kinship there were shattered!
Exhausted he was led to a cold-blooded death,
A prisoner in bonds walking like a hobbled beast . . .'

[38] Al-Tabari, *The Commentary on the Qur'an*, Vol.1, p.48.

were killed. The vanquished accepted both Islam and the Qur'an brought by the Prophet Muhammad.[39] The casualties were also very heavy among the Muslim armies, and included some of those who were said to have known part or all of the Qur'an by heart. It is usually reported that this slaughter of Muslims first gave rise to the idea of collecting an official written version of the Qur'an into one volume.[40]

Outwardly the remaining followers of Musaylima had become Muslims but some of them were still secretly loyal to Musaylima, even though he was officially labelled a liar, *Kadha'ab*, by the Muslim hierarchy. Khurshid, quoting *Sunan Kubra* and *Kanzul umall*, states that Abdullah Ibn Masood (who was an official teacher of the Qur'an in Kufa) came to know about a group of the Banu Hunaifa who acknowledged the prophethood of Musaylima and sang his praises. Ibn Masood seized them and made a complaint to the Caliph Uthman. The order received from the Caliph was: 'Call these people to revert to Islam; invite them to affirm the *Shahada*. Those who repent from Musaylima and accept this invitation, spare them. Those who would still stand with Musaylima, slay them.'[41]

Musaylima is said to have had acknowledged Muhammad as a prophet but claimed partnership in his prophethood. He used to utter rhymes in *saj*[42] and speak in

---

[39] Abdul Haqq, *Madarij-e-Nabbuwat*, (Urdu tr), part 2, pp.687–689.

[40] *Sahih al-Bukhari*, Vol. 6, p.477.

[41] Khurshid Ahmad Khurshid, *Hazrat Usman Ke Sarkari Khatoot*, p.139.

[42] Some believe that the text of the Qur'an is in rhymed prose, known as *Saj'*. This form was well known among the pre-Islamic poets of Arabia. *Saj'* has no consistent rhythmic or metrical pattern, but shares with poetry the element of rhyme

imitation of the style of the Qur'an.[43] Imam Razi, in his commentary on Surah 6:93, 'Who can be more wicked than one who inventeth a lie against Allah, or said, "I have received inspiration", when he hath received none, or (again) who saith, "I can reveal the like of what Allah hath revealed?"', states that this verse was revealed regarding Musaylima and al-Aswad al-Ansi.

Tafsir Ibn Kathir in its comments on Surah 2 states that Umro bin Al-A's was once asked by Musaylima about any succinct and eloquent Surah revealed to Muhammad. Al-A's recited the Surah *al-Asr*. On hearing this, Musaylima paused for a while with his head down and then, raising it, he recited a similar Surah of his own. Some of his work is still available, but critics express doubts whether Musaylima was indeed the source of the sayings attributed to him. They could be later inventions intended to brand him as a clumsy imitator.

Al-Aswad Al-Ansi

A similar claim of prophethood to that mentioned above was made by *Al-Ansi*, a man in San'a. His substantial following believed that he had received revelations. When Al-Mughara went to San'a to collect *Sadaqat* offerings, he caused a considerable insurrection in the south of Arabia. According to Baladhuri he had claimed to be a prophet on behalf of God, the *Rahman*.[44] Both Abu Jafar al-Tabari (d.923) in his *Tarikh al-Tabari* and Abul fidah (d.1331) in his *Tarikh Abul fidah* express the official line that Al-Ansi was

---

[42] (*continued*) known as *fasila* (pl. *fawasil*) and it is that feature which we find in the Qur'an. For a detailed study on *fawasil* and *Saj'* see Suyuti, *Itqan*, Vol. 2, pp.239–261; Subhi Salih, *Ulum al-Qur'an*, p.466.

[43] Ibn Hisham, p.637.

[44] Gibb and Kramers, *Shorter Encyclopaedia of Islam*, p.49.

an expert in trickery and sweet talk, and he used both to attract his listeners.

The popular claim is that these people 'were not able, and eventually confessed to their incapacity' to bring a like of the Qur'an.[45] Our study, however, shows that these people were defeated not because their 'words' were poor when compared with the Qur'an but because they could not gather a sufficient military following to face the Muslim threat.

Ibn al-Muqaffa and *Abul-Ala al-Marri*

Ibn al-Muqaffa was a prominent Arabic prose writer who is said to have tried to imitate the Qur'an. He was put to death in 756.[46] Some believe that the Syrian poet and thinker Abul-Ala al-Marri (d.1058) wrote his *Kitabul Fusul wa'l-ghayat* in imitation of, and aiming to excel the Qur'an in its *ijaz*. He considered some of his own writings to be on a par with the Qur'an.[47] Some critics, however, doubt whether Marri intended his work to be an imitation.

Bab, the founder of Babi which survives today as *Bahai*, believed that he was called by God to replace Muhammad as the prophet and to replace Islam with a new religion. His work, *Bayan* is a statement of this new faith, based on revelations from God. He asserted that his work *Tafsir Surat Yusuf* was the same Qur'an which was originally revealed to Muhammad. He was publicly executed in 1850 after about three years of imprisonment.

---

[45] *Roots of religion*, p.146.
[46] Rippin, *Approaches to the History of the Interpretation of the Qur'an*, p.212–213.
[47] Dashti, *Twenty Three Years*, p.48. See also *The Encyclopaedia of Islam*, Vol.v, p.932.

The Jinn

It is usually argued that if all people and all the *jinn* were to gather to produce something like the verses of the Qur'an, they would not be able to do it (Surah 17:88). However, as discussed earlier, some people *were* able to imitate and write like the Qur'an. As for the jinn, the majority of Muslims declare Satan to be one of the jinn. Several Muslim historians and commentators relate that one day while the prophet was reciting *Surah al-Najam*[48] (Surah 53: 19–20), Satan caused him to add, 'These (the idols Lat and Uzza etc.) are the exalted beauties whose intercession may indeed be hoped for.'[49] Though Al-Ghazali, Baihaqi and today's modern commentators of the Qur'an reject the story, it is confirmed and recorded by other Muslims like Suyuti, Hafiz Ibn Hajar, Ibn Kathir, Baidhawi, Zamakhshari, Ibn Hisham and Tabari. In the light of their comments it would mean that not only was Satan able to make a verse like the Qur'anic ones but that he was either able to compel Muhammad to recite it as part of the Qur'an or that Muhammad was not able to tell the difference between the Qur'anic revelations from the two sources, Allah and Satan. In his commentary, *Kashshaf*, Zamakhshari asserts that this episode which Muhammad experienced is common knowledge and unquestionable, and is related by the companions of Muhammad.[50]

Surah al-Wilayah and Surah an-Nurain

Among the writings of Shia scholarship, we find two Surahs *al-Wilayah* and *an-Nurain* which are believed by

---

[48] Some seem to suggest that it was Surah 22:51.
[49] al-Razi's *Tafsir al-Kabir* on Surah 22:52.
[50] Zamakhshari, *Al-Kashshaf*, Part 3, pp.164–165.

سورة الولايت سبع آيات

بـــــم الله الرحمٰن الرحيم

يـآءِيُّهَا الذِينَ اٰمَنُوا بالنَّبِى وبالوَلِى
الذَّينِ بَعثناهُما يَهدِياٰنِكُم الى صِراطٍ مُستقيم، نَبِيٌّ
وَوَلِيٌّ بَعضُهُما مِنْ بَعْضٍ وانَا العَلِيم الخَبِيرُ. ان
الذِينَ يُؤمِنُونَ بِعَهدِ الله لهم جنَّات النَّعِيم. وَالذِينَ
اِذا تُلِيتْ عَلَيهم اٰيٰتُنا كانُوا بِاٰيٰتِنا مُكَذِّبِين.ان
لهُم فى جَهنَّم مقامًا عظِيمًا اِذَا نُودِىَ لهُم يَومَ
القِياٰمةِ اَيْنَ الضَّالِمُون المُكَذِّبُون للمُرسَلِين. مَا خَلَفَهُم
المُرسَلِين اِلا بالحَقّ وَمَا كانَ الله لِيُظْهِرَهُم اِلى
اَجَلٍ قَرِيب. وَسَبِّح بِحَمدِ رَبِّكَ وَعَلِيٌّ مِنَ الشّاهِدِينَ.

Figure 17. Surah al-Wilayah

This Surah although not included in the present Qur'an is believed by some prominent Shia Muslims to be part of it.

some to be part of the Qur'an but which have been rejected by Sunni *Ulema*. The style and oration is similar to that of the Qur'an. A copy of the Surah *al-Wilayah* and a few verses of *an-Nurain* are as illustrated.

The *Ijaz al-Qur'an*

It is interesting to know that among Muslims there have been men of learning who have rejected the *Ijaz* formula. According to some earlier sects like *Mutazila* and *Nizamiah,* people were capable of writing something like the Qur'an. Abu Musa, known as Al-Murdar (d.841)

سورة النورين إثنين و اربعين آية

بسم الله الرحمن الرحيم

يا أيها الذين آمنوا آمنوا بالنورين اللذين أنزلناهما يتلوان عليكم آياتي وبحذرانكم عذاب يوم عظيم ۞ نوران بعضهما من بعض وإني لسميع عليم ۞ إن الذين يوفون بعهد الله ورسوله في آيات لهم جنات نعيم ۞ والذين كفروا من بعد ما آمنوا بنقضهم ميثاقهم وما عاهدهم الرسول عليهم يعذبون في الجحيم ۞ ظلموا أنفسهم وعتوا لوصي الرسول أولئك يسقون من حميم ۞ إن الله الذي نور السموات والأرض بما شاء واصطفى من الملائكة والرسل وجعل من المؤمنين ۞ أولئك من خلقه يفعل الله ما يشاء لا إله إلا هو الرحمن الرحيم ۞ قد مكر الذين من قبلهم برسلهم فأخذتهم بمكرهم إن أخذي شديد أليم ۞ إن الله قد أهلك عادا وثمود بما كسبوا وجعلهم لكم تذكرة فلا تتقون ۞ وفرعون بما طغى على موسى وأخيه هارون أغرقته ومن تبعه أجمعين ۞ ليكون لكم آية وإن أكثركم فاسقون ۞ إن الله يجمعهم يوم المحشر

Figure 18. Surah an-Nurain

A few verses from Surah Nurain which has 42 verses. Although some Muslims quietly accept the whole chapter as part of the Qur'an, the majority reject it. The style, diction and oration is similar to that of the Qur'an.

maintained that 'man is able to (produce) something like the Qur'an as regards the purity of its language, its arrangement and eloquence.'[51] Similarly Ibrahim an-Nazzam (d.835) believed that 'Muhammad's pagan adversaries were not permanently incapable of producing anything linguistically comparable to his revelation, but temporarily "averted" from using their rhetorical and poetical skill (sarfa).'[52] Others, such as Hisham b. Amr al-Fuwati (died between 842 and 847) and Abad b. Sulayman

---

[51] *The Encyclopaedia of Islam*, Vol. vii, p.604.
[52] *The Encyclopaedia of Islam*, Vol. vii, p.1058.

(d.864), have also acknowledged openly that the Qur'an was not miraculous in its syntax and that work of equal value could be produced by other people.

Conclusion

Muslims claim for the Qur'an what it does not claim for itself. The claim that God prevented people from imitating the Qur'an is very difficult to sustain. If this view is to be believed, then the challenge is meaningless.

The Arabs did not aim to outdo the Qur'an, because it was a miracle, but because they did not believe in most of its theology. Some imitated its narrative style concerning stories of people gone by. Later people remained silent for fear of persecution, as can be seen from Uthman's attitude to the group which still honoured Musaylima.

The language, the style, the rhetoric and the eloquence of the Qur'an do indeed have their own special place, but they have been exaggerated. The passages that contain the challenge of inimitability should be understood not only within their textual context, but also in the context of their historical setting. The Qur'an, like the Bible, was written in the living language of people of the time, in this case in 7th century Arabia. Like other languages, its composition is bound by rules and subject to interpretation. Although the structure of Arabic language and its composition is very much moulded by the Qur'an, critics still find grammatical mistakes in it and point to the fact that its literary style and manner, narratives and teachings are not unique or inimitable. On the other hand generally Muslims hold on to their view stating, 'The Qur'an is the best old Arabic we have – all other Arabic self-consciously follows it in terms of style and syntax.' The Qur'an is therefore *defined* as the best!

9

The supremacy of the Scriptures

When deadlock is reached in Muslim/Christian discussions concerning the integrity of the Bible, some Muslims move on to the argument that even if it is accepted that the integrity of the Bible is trustworthy, this book is now *mansukh* – abrogated, annulled, repealed, abolished. It is claimed that the Qur'an has replaced and superseded it: the Qur'an is now God's final Testament and the only perfect Revelation; all that was good in the Bible is now contained in the Qur'an.

> Every prophet who was in the days of Moses and after him was upon the highroad of Moses and his religious law and obedient to his book, until the time of Jesus. And every Prophet who was in the days of Jesus and after Him was upon the road of Jesus and his religious laws and obedient to his book, until the time of our prophet Muhammad. And the religious law of Muhammad shall not be abrogated until the day of the Resurrection.[1]

To reinforce this theory, some recent Muslim commentators interpret those verses of the Qur'an which declare that the Torah and Injil have *guidance and light*, in the past

---

[1] Pfander, *Mizan ul Haqq*, p.56.

tense (as mentioned in chapter 6), thus stating, 'there *was* light and guidance in them.'

Al-Naskh Wa al-Mansukh: The theory of abrogation

Does the Qur'an really claim to have abrogated the previous Scriptures? Abrogation means to invalidate, to annul or to remove the effect. In the Qur'an the verb *nasakha* (with the sense *to abrogate*) occurs in only two places:

> Such of Our revelations as we abrogate or cause to be forgotten, we bring (in place) one better or the like thereof. Knowest thou not that Allah is able to do all things? (Surah 2:106)

> Never sent we a messenger or a Prophet before thee but when he recited (the message) Satan proposed (opposition) in respect of that which he recited thereof. But Allah abolisheth that which Satan proposeth. Then Allah establisheth His revelations. Allah is knower, wise. (Surah 22:51)

Suyuti in his *Asbab al-Nuzul* quotes Ibn Abbas as saying, 'Sometimes the revelation used to descend on the prophet during the night and then he would forget it during the daytime, thus God sent this verse (Surah 2:106).'

Muslim scholars from the classical period have collected lists of abrogating and abrogated verses from the Qur'an (which obviously helps to explain away conflicting verses, for example, Surah 2:256 and 10:100; Surah 3:85 and 2:161; Surah 23:96 and 5:13; Surah 9:5 and 29:30). But these lists rarely agree. Now, if the theory of abrogation is to apply only to the previous Scriptures (i.e. the Bible), then where is the general Muslim consensus to this effect?

What are Muslims to do about the conflicting verses in the Qur'an? The fact is that in spite of these methods and the many lists available from the doctors of Islam, the doctrine of abrogation does not adequately deal with the conflict between verses within the Qur'an, let alone abrogate the Bible.

The substitution of one revelation for another

> And when we put a revelation in place of (another) revelation – and Allah knoweth best what He revealeth – they say: Lo! thou art but inventing. Most of them know not. (Surah 16:101)

Some Muslims claim that the Arabic word *ayah* (verse) in this and other passages (Surah 2:106; 13:39 and 22:51) 'refers not to the text of Qur'an itself, but to previous Scriptures including the Torah and the Gospel'.[2] The majority of Muslim exegetes agree that these passages refer to the abrogation of some passages of the Qur'an. We learn from the same source about the background of this passage that Muhammad was accused by his opponents of giving contradictory statements in the Qur'an. As a result, he is said to have received a revelation that Allah replaced some of the text with a later text. Furthermore, this verse does not state that Allah replaced one *'Kitab'* (book) with another but rather that he substituted one *ayah* for another. The word *ayah* also means 'sign'. However in the context of this passage and others (Surah 2:106; 13:39 and 22:51) it refers only to the verses of the Qur'an and not the book of the Christians or the Jews.

The theory of *Naskh* is not confined just to verses of the Qur'an, but is said to affect the Sunnah. However, we find

---

[2] Kamali, *Principles of Islamic Jurisprudence*, p.163.

'no early scholar suggested that the root *ayah* might refer to anything other than to a verse of the Qur'an.'[3] We see prominent and respected Muslim scholars of Islam admit that the Qur'an is both the abrogator and the abrogated. According to al-Shafi (d.767) the matter of abrogation, *al-Naskh* 'is a wholly internal phenomenon of the Qur'an.'[4] Among other people holding a similar view are Abu Ubaid Qasim Bin Salam, Abu Dawud Sajistani, Abu Jaffar Nuhaas, Ibn Al-Anbari and Jalal al-Din Suyuti. In his famous scholarly book, *'Al Itqan fi Ulum al-Qur'an'*, in chapter 47 on the subject of *'Naskh Wa-l-mansukh fi al-Qur'an'*, Suyuti writes that abrogation is something which God has only favoured the Muslims with. He gives details of various stages of abrogation and then lists those Qur'anic verses which are abrogated by other verses of the Qur'an. He also lists verses which are said to be abrogated but for which a replacement text is not available.[5]

The following traditions, for example, from Islamic sources certainly prove our point that the Islamic doctrine of abrogation is an internal affair of Islamic revelation and does not extend to include the Bible: Abdullah Ibn Masood relates that Muhammad one day recited a verse, which Masood immediately wrote down. The next day he found it had vanished from the material on which he had written it. He told Muhammad about this and thus they came to know that God had revoked that particular verse.

According to another tradition, Ibn Umar is related to have said, 'Two men read a Surah which the apostle of God had taught them, yet one night they rose up to pray but they failed to remember one word of it. The next morning, they went to the apostle of God and related it to him.

---

[3] Burton, *Abu Ubaid al-Qasim b. Sallam's Kitab al-nasikh wa-l-mansukh*, p.13.

[4] Kamali, *Principles of Islamic Jurisprudence*, p.159.

[5] Suyuti, *Al-Itqan fi Ulum al-Qur'an*, Vol. 2, pp.52–69.

He told them, "It is one of those which have been abrogated, thus, forget about it."[6]

Authorities differ as to the number of verses abrogated. Some say two hundred and twenty, yet others go down to as few as five. For example while al-Suyuti has claimed twenty-one instances of Naskh in the Qur'an, Shah Wali Allah (d.1762) retained only five of those cases as genuine.[7]

Shaikh Al-Hajj Rahmatullah (d.1891), a Muslim protagonist and acclaimed debater of the 19th century, wrote in Arabic against Jewish and Christian teachings in his book *Izharul Haqq*. There are revised translations available in Urdu[8] and English[9] which are currently used by Muslims in their discussions with Christians. Although he wrote against the Bible, he believed that the idea that the Qur'an has abrogated the earlier books is wrong. 'The saying that the Torah has been abrogated by the Psalms and the Psalms by the Gospel has no basis either in the Qur'an or in the Commentaries.'[10]

In the 19th century the famous Muslim, Sir Syed Ahmad Khan (d.1898), whose pioneer work, *Tafsir al-Qur'an* was intended to bring Islam and modern educational systems together, wrote in his *Commentary on the Holy Bible*, 'Those who imagine it to be part of the Muhammadan creed that one law has totally repealed another are utterly mistaken. We hold no such doctrine.'[11]

---

[6] Suyuti, *Al-Itqan fi Ulum al-Qur'an*, Vol. 2, p.66.

[7] Kamali, Muhammad Hashim, *Principles of Islamic Jurisprudence*, p.162.

[8] Izharul Haqq (Urdu) *Bible say Qur'an Tak*, (4 volumes) Karachi: Darul Ulum, n.d.

[9] *Izharul Haqq*, (English), 4 Volumes, London: Taha Publishers, 1989.

[10] Pfander, *Mizan ul Haqq*, p.58.

[11] Syed Ahmad Khan, *Commentary on the Holy Bible*, Vol 1, p.268, cited in *The Faith of Islam*, p.89.

Confirmation, not abrogation

If the Qur'an does not abrogate the earlier books, then what is its relation to them? The Qur'an, a Muslim's first and most important authority, does not suggest that previous Scriptures were ever abrogated. As mentioned elsewhere, the Qur'an claims to be confirming what went before it *(musadiqallima bayna yadayhi)*, namely the Tawrat and Injil (Surah 3:3). At another place it gives the news to Jews and Christians that it came to confirm what they possess *(musadiqallima makum)* (Surah 4:47).

If the Qur'an had abrogated the earlier Scriptures, how could it ask the Jews and Christians to follow their Scriptures (Surah 5:43,47,68). In fact the Qur'an says that if they don't judge according to the Torah then they are among the *Kafiroon*, disbelievers: 'Whoso judgeth not by which Allah hath revealed: such are disbelievers' (Surah 5:44).

No categorical statement

Some Muslims claim that the Qur'an has superseded the previous Scriptures because it has clear, precise, and detailed commandments and instructions for each and every thing. They base their argument on the passages where the Qur'an claims to be *kitaben mubin*, a book which puts things in clear perspective (Surah 26:2) and *ahsanat tafsir*, the best explanation (Surah 25:33).

It could be argued in the light of the claim that the Qur'an being *mubin* and *ahsanat tafsir*, that it has superseded and abrogated the Bible, but in no way has it clearly stated such abrogation. Instead of saying, *'O People of the Book! Ye have no ground to stand upon unless ye stand fast by the Torah and the Gospel'* (Surah 5:68), the Qur'an should have said, 'O people of the Book! Ye have no ground to stand upon unless ye stand fast by the Qur'an instead of the Torah and the Gospel which it has abrogated.' Yet the Qur'an, which claims to have clear instructions, does not say so. Instead it says about the Torah and Injil, *wafihi huddan wa noorun* – in them there is guidance and light (Surah 5:46) and *fiha hukmallah* – therein is the (plain) command of Allah (Surah 5:43).

Asbab-un-Nuzul, the reason for revelation

Some Muslims state that God sent the Qur'an and it abrogated the earlier Scriptures because the Jews and Christians had made many changes in them. To support the theory of corruption in the Bible (and the abrogation of it) they refer to several verses of the Qur'an where the word *tahrif*, alteration, appears as *Yuharrifuna* (they alter). In one or two other verses another word *badala*, to change, as *Yubadilonahu* (they change) is used (Surah 4:46; 5:13; 5:41; 2:75). However, study of the background and the reason of *asbab-un-nuzul* for these passages in the Qur'an and in the Ahadith reveal as already mentioned before in Chapter 5 that the local Jews deliberately used to misquote both their Scripture and Muhammad's revelation or decision. Sometimes they brought questions to him to answer. They would even pretend that they had no information in the Torah to decide on a matter and then later make fun of Muhammad, saying that if he were a messenger of God, he would have seen through their mischievous plans. Hence the passages condemning them are found in the Qur'an.

Ahluz-zekr, the learned men

The Qur'an states: 'And if thou (Muhammad) art in doubt concerning that which we reveal unto thee, then question those who read the Scripture (that was) before thee . . .' (Surah 10:94). Such a suggestion from God to Muhammad would never have been made if the earlier Scriptures were corrupted or abrogated in the way some Muslims now think they are. The opinions of the *Ahluz-zekr*, the learned men of the Torah and the Injil spoken of in the Qur'an, should be considered especially when hard questions arise. A similar suggestion is also mentioned in Surah 16:43. These verses show that the Qur'an did not come to abrogate the previous Scriptures.

The Qur'an: the final testament?

Some Muslims believe that the 'Qur'an has come not only to abrogate all previous Scriptures; for, in view of the changed condition of mankind, it has brought a new *Sharia* (Law), which is not only better than all the codes of Law, but is also meant for all men and all times.'[12] To propagate this belief, there are Muslims in the West today who call the Qur'an 'The Final Testament.' Some Islamic missions in their adverts and propagation material use slogans like, 'Read the Qur'an, The Last Testament'. Rashad Khalifa has titled his translation of the Qur'an as, '*Qur'an: The Final Testament* (Authorised English Version).[13] Others advertise the Qur'an as, *The Future World Constitution*, which they claim has abrogated the Old and the New Testament. Some claim that one day the whole world will be one nation under one *Sharia*, that is, the law of Islam. Addressing the *al-Muhajiroon* rally on the 8th September

---

[12] *The Holy Qur'an with English Translation and Commentary*, Vol. 1, p.164.
[13] Rashad Khalifa, *Qur'an: The Final Testament* (Authorised English Version), 1992.

1996 in Hyde Park, the ex-leader of *Hizbut-tahrir,* now the leader of the *al-Muhajiroon* movement, Sheikh Omar Bakri Muhammad, claimed that one day Britain and the whole world would be governed by Islamic law.[14] Unfortunately for them, the Qur'an has a different view.

The word *Testament* means covenant (see Chapter 1). In Arabic it translates *Ahd* or *Mithaq.* In the Bible, Genesis to Revelation, there are frequent references to the Abrahamic and Mosaic covenants/testaments, and then there is the new testament or covenant with Jesus, all explicitly recorded in the Old Testament, *Al Ahdul Qadim* and the New Testament, *Al, Ahdul Jadid.* However, nowhere in the Qur'an are any phrases used which are akin to 'the final testament', *Al-Ahdul Akhir* or *Al-Ahdul Ukhra.* Nowhere does it call itself 'the last testament'.

The Qur'an itself refutes the suggestion that one day the whole world will be one nation under the one constitution, one law. The Qur'an says, 'For each We have appointed a divine law and a traced-out way. Had Allah willed He could have made you one community. But that He may try you by that which He hath given you' (Surah 5:48).[15] In other words, according to the Qur'an, the Muslim's first hand authority, God has appointed for each group a law and a way. His purpose appears to be that each faith community will be judged by the revelation it has received.

One religion?

The Qur'an claims (and Muslims also affirm) that the religion or *Din* which Muhammad brought is the same as that

[14] Daily *Jang,* London: September 9, 1996, pp.1 and 12.

[15] Pickthall, *The Meaning of the Glorious Koran,* (Delhi, Taj Company, 1989).

brought by Abraham, Moses and Jesus. If this Islamic belief is to make any sense, it is meaningless to say that the Qur'an has abrogated the Torah, the Psalms, the Books of the Prophets and the Gospel. The Qur'an states, 'Say (O Muslim): We believe in Allah and that which is revealed unto us and that which was revealed unto Abraham, and Ishmael, and Isaac, and that which Moses and Jesus received, and that which the Prophets received from their Lord. We make no distinction between any of them, and unto him we have surrendered' (Surah 2:136). This would mean that a Muslim is required to believe in the *Shariah* of the Prophets which came before the Qur'an and make no distinction between any of them. This emphasis makes the whole idea of abrogation of the earlier Scriptures and replacement by the Qur'an wholly contradictory.

Answers to everything?

Some Muslims claim that the Qur'an has answers to everything. It contains all necessary knowledge from within the previous Scriptures. If that is the case, should one say then that the biblical accounts of prophets like Isaiah, Jeremiah, Daniel, Ezekiel and other prophets should simply be dismissed as irrelevant because the Qur'an does not include them in its passages? No, certainly not. There is guidance in them. They contain a warning of God's wrath, and the news of his judgement, reminding people that when God's people do not behave the way they should, he is not too far away to punish them.

If the Qur'an had answers to everything, then would there be any need of the huge collections of traditions, the Hadith? If the Qur'an was both clear and comprehensive, as some Muslims claim, then a seeker would not need to go into the details of the *Ulum al-Qur'an wal Hadith wal*

Fiqh, the science of the Qur'an, the traditions and the long development of Islamic jurisprudence.

Some Muslims say that the Qur'an contains minimal but succinct information of all that is good in the previous books. But is this accurate? Does the Qur'an claim this for itself? It does not. If *minimal* information were all that is necessary, the Qur'an would not have constantly repeated many of its teachings, accounts and events in its pages. For example, the argument between God and Satan in Surah 7 is repeated in Surah 38. Adam's story is available to us in Surah 2 and repeated in Surah 20. Prophet Hud's address is mentioned in Surah 7, repeated with additions and some omissions in Surah 11 and Surah 26. Similarly, the prophet Shuaib is in Surah 7, repeated in Surah 11, and then in Surah 26 and Surah 29. Moses and the Exodus of the Israelites are found in at least eight places.

Conclusion

The Qur'an does not claim that Allah replaced one *Kitab* (book) with another, but rather that he substituted one passage for another within the Qur'an. The key verses of the Qur'an in support for the doctrine of abrogation refer only to the verses of the Qur'an and not to the Scriptures of Christians or Jews. A Muslim has to make no distinction between the Qur'an and previous books. This makes the whole idea of the Bible being abrogated irrational. There is no passage in the Qur'an either to abrogate the Scriptures of the Jews and Christians or to warrant a departure from them. In fact the Qur'an, on the whole, confirms the Torah and the Injil. The Qur'an does not have an answer to everything as is popularly claimed. The *Sunnah*, *Qiyas*, *Ijma* etc. were needed as secondary sources for Islamic thought and practice.

10

Epilogue

Everything that has a beginning has an end and this book is no different. I realise that some of what I have written may have displeased some readers. Scholars may disapprove and criticise me for not being sufficiently scholarly, while others may accuse me of being too academic. Some may criticise me for being very soft in my approach and yet others for being too harsh. I expect it all. I have tried not to denigrate anyone's faith but to question the standards by which I believe most Muslims and Christians assess the integrity of each other's Scriptures.

A recapitulation

We will briefly look back to remind ourselves what this book is all about. We saw that both Muslims and Christians believe that their Scriptures are inspired and preserved (Chapter 1). Documentary evidence shows that whereas the message has indeed been preserved, both books have suffered from editing errors and some variants in the text. Christians are very open about this matter. Information of variations in the biblical text can be found reproduced in most of the modern translations available to us. In contrast we find that the present translations and commentaries of the Qur'an are silent about *its* variants and omissions. One has to go to the classical writings of Muslim scholars to obtain such information (chapters 2 and 5). We learn that the histories of the compiling of the Qur'an and the Bible have many similarities.

Has the Bible been corrupted in such a way that it cannot be trusted? The testimony of the Qur'an itself says otherwise. We found how it affirms the reliability of the Christian and Jewish Scriptures (Chapter 4) and that they were available in a trustworthy form at the time of Muhammad, who consulted them.

The Qur'an also says that no one can change the Word of God. If the Jews (and Christians) *did* corrupt the Word of God, then it would mean that the Qur'anic statement is unreliable, which would be blasphemy to Muslims. The conclusion in the light of the Qur'an and later historical evidence must be to trust that copies of the earlier Scriptures were available in Makkah and Madinah and that they were the same as those available today. Since Christians have unassailable documentary evidence from before Muhammad's time, they can confidently claim that their Scriptures *are* trustworthy (Chapter 3).

The question of contradictions in the Bible was considered in Chapter 5, and it was seen that most of the objections could easily be answered and the problems solved in the light of context and background. Certain passages may be difficult to explain; however, similar problems also arise in the Qur'an. The question of corruption in translations of both the Bible and the Qur'an was also addressed. We saw how easily the evaluation criterion which is used against the Bible could just as effectively be used against the Qur'an to highlight the same sort of shortcomings as are found in the Bible. If such frailties do not affect the integrity of the Qur'an, then there should be no problem when dealing with the Bible.

Some Muslims argue that the Qur'an does not confirm what Christians have today as Scriptures. The evidence of the Qur'an and the biblical documents show that the Scriptures which are available today are the same as those of Muhammad's time. We dealt with statements like: 'The Bible is unknown to the Qur'an; there was only one Injil and since Christians do not have the Gospel in the original Aramaic, it is not trustworthy' (Chapter 6).

We investigated the debate over the Qur'anic word *tahrif* and also looked through some of the internal and circumstantial evidence for the Scriptures available at the time of Muhammad. We made a detailed analysis of the several Muslim objections and comments to show that the tests some Muslims use against the Bible also condemn the Qur'an.

Looking at the facts, it must be concluded that we have in our hands the very Scriptures which the Qur'an declares to be *huddan lin-nas*, a guidance for the people. The study of the Qur'an, the Bible and their history shows that there have been many disagreements among theologians and critics. If there are said to be reasons to believe that the present Bible does not contain the whole of the message, then the same can also be said of the present Qur'an (Chapter 5). Just as there may be lost verses of the Bible, the same can be said of the Qur'an. If the Bible is discredited because a human element was part of its revelation then, again, the same can be said of the Qur'an (Chapter 5). Looking at what the companions of Muhammad and, later, the great authors of Islam have said about the Qur'an, one can confidently come to the conviction that the history of the compilation of the Qur'an involves just as much of a human element. On both sides we learn of editing and recension.

If it said that there simply have been some among Christians accusing others of misquoting and alteration of the Scriptures, indeed there have been Muslims against Muslims accusing each other of the same offence. In spite of such a situation if Muslims believe that the Qur'an has come through, so do Christians believe that the Bible has survived such onslaughts. Both Muslims and Christians would agree that one must dismiss the wilder claims of dissident groups of either faith.

We showed in Chapter 7 that the so-called Gospel of Barnabas is a medieval forgery which contradicts the Qur'an as much as the Bible. To assert the superiority of the Qur'an over the Bible, Muslims claim that the Qur'an is inimitable and that it has superseded the previous Scriptures (Chapter 8). However, we saw that such a belief brings its own problems and side effects. To say that no one was able to respond to the challenge of the Qur'an contradicts what we learn from Islamic sources.

With regard to abrogation and the Bible being super-seded by the Qur'an, we saw that such a doctrine has no support in the Islamic Scripture (Chapter 9). While the Qur'an does talk about abrogation, this only relates to parts of its own revelation and not to the previous Scriptures which it claims to have come to confirm.

Points to ponder

The messages of both the Bible and the Qur'an are well preserved. Instead of arguing about their integrity, we should be listening, comparing and analysing what these books have to say. Why talk about God, prophethood and the hereafter. Why is God so interested in us? Why has he been sending his guidance to us? What do these books say about what we are as humans and where we are heading?

What is life, death, God, mercy and salvation, now and in the hereafter?

Both Muslims and Christians pray repeatedly for the forgiveness of their sins, and God's mercy. They hope one day to be accepted into his paradise. The question should therefore be of salvation, *Najah*. Can we have assurance of it in this life? Can we get this assurance by believing and keeping a set of rules or is there something beyond which may give us assurance in this life of being accepted into paradise in the light of the teachings in the Bible or the Qur'an? Both Muslims and Christians should be considering and sharing what their respective Scriptures have to *say* about these fundamental questions which are more important than to indulge in an endless 'battle of books' especially when the vital matters of eternal life or death are at stake.

Appendix

Apocryphal writings

In their discussions with Christians, some Muslims suggest that certain collections of literature, described as 'apocryphal' cast doubt on the biblical canon, and thus the present Bible cannot be taken as authentic.[1] They ask why the Roman Catholics and Greek Orthodox appear to believe in them but they are ignored by other Christian groups?

It should be emphasised that in the New Testament all Christians accept the same canonical books. The alleged controversy is only over the apocryphal writings associated with the Old Testament.

The term *Apocrypha* (Greek: *apokryphos*) means hidden, veiled. Today the word is applied to fourteen or fifteen books that are found in some Old Testament manuscripts like the Greek Septuagint but not in the accepted Hebrew texts. The apocryphal writings were not universally accepted by the early Christians, nor were they part of the Hebrew Canon of Scripture. The main reason for this was that these writings appeared long after the era of the prophets. Though some of them bore, as their alleged authors, the names of some notable men in Hebrew history, this was not sufficient to consider them as part of the

---

[1] Bilal Philips, p.20.

Hebrew Scriptures, known to Christians as the Old Testament.

Most of these books were not originally written in Hebrew (the main language for the Hebrew Scriptures), so Jewish leaders did not regard them as inspired. This conclusion was confirmed by the Jewish Council of Jamnia (90 CE). The Roman Catholic Church officially declared them to be part of the Old Testament but with the lesser status as 'Apocrypha' only about four hundred years ago, at the Council of Trent (1545–1563). This acceptance was to a great extent a reaction to the Protestant reformation.

Furthermore, some of the writers of this body of literature denied having inspiration (1 Maccabees 4:46; 9:27; 2 Maccabees 2:33). The existence of these writings in Greek translations of the Hebrew Bible of Jesus' time did not mean they were regarded as essential or inspired. The majority of early Christian fathers agreed with the Jewish conclusions when they considered these books. While some of them quoted from these books, none of them gave them canonical status thereby emphasising their lower status.

In other contexts, some Muslims and others refer to the Syriac Church of the fourth century to point out its integrity. It is notable, however, that the Peshitta, the Syriac collection of the Scriptures of the second century did not contain any of the apocryphal literature. Some people infer that Jerome (d.420) must have accepted the Apocrypha as canonical when he revised the translation of the Old Latin Bible. However, Jerome was merely revising. He was careful in his own translation of the Old Testament, and regarded his own time as too valuable to be spent on translating uninspired writings.[2] While at one stage

---

[2] James Hastings (Ed.), *Dictionary of the Bible*, pp.41–42.

Augustine (d.430) did acknowledge them (in part), he later gave a clear rejection of them, and treated them as outside the canon, and inferior to the Hebrew Scriptures.[3] The Christian view of these writings has always been that they contained useful examples of God's, dealings with his people, but that they contain no essential teaching which is not found in the canonical books.[4]

---

[3] McDowell, *Answers to Tough Questions about the Christian Faith*, p.38.
[4] Colin Brown (Ed.), *New International Dictionary of New Testament Theology*, Vol. 1, p.50.

Glossary

Ahl al-Kitab: (*Ahl-ul-Kitab*) the people of the Book, Jews and Christians.

Apocrypha: (Greek: apokryphos) means hidden, veiled. The word is synonymous with a body of literature (fourteen or fifteen books), that is part of some late Old Testament manuscripts like the Greek Septuagint but not the Hebrew Old Testament.

Archetype: text written out by a professional scribe and the form in which the work was published. All copies derive from this.

Autograph: the original author's manuscript in his own handwriting, from which is produced the Archetype.

Baitulmal: the treasury.

Caliph: successor of the Prophet and head of the Islamic community.

Canon: literally a 'measuring rod'. Refers to the list of books regarded by the Church as composing its Scriptures. 'Canonical' therefore means 'having the status of Scripture' or 'included in the canon'.

Codex: (pl. codices) leaf-form of book. Superseded the roll-form around second century CE.

Commentary: extended explanation of a text.

Da'wah: literally means invite or inform. Muslim evangelism, edification.

Din: religion.

Exempler: the art of explaining the text by means of a commentary intended to describe the author's meaning.

Exemplar: manuscript from which a copy is transcribed.

Father (church): a theological writer or commentator of the early Church. Most of them wrote in Greek or Latin, a few in Syriac.

Fatwa: (pl. *fatawa*), an opinion on Islamic law given by a Mufti; collected legal opinions from a corpus which modifies the application of the early codes of Islamic law.

Fiqh: understanding, jurisprudence, Islamic law.

Hadith: a report of sayings or deeds of Muhammad transmitted by his companions; collections of *hadith* are second in authority to the Qur'an as the source of Muslim belief and practice.

Hajj: the annual pilgrimage to Makkah.

Hijrah: the migration of the Muslims in 622 CE from Makkah to Madina.

Ijma: consensus of legal scholars or of the community as a whole; a basis of Muslim law.

Ikhtiar: the right of choice.

Imam: the religious leader of the community;
                          the successor to the Prophet, used com-
                          monly by the Shia for Ali and his
                          descendants.

Injil: the New Testament part of the Bible.

Isnad: a chain of authorities, the series of
                          transmitters of hadith whose names
                          authenticate their validity.

Jinn: class of spirits in Muslim theology;
                          invisible beings, either harmful or
                          helpful (sing. *jinni*).

Ka'ba: the central sanctuary of Islam, located
                          in Makkah, the principal object of *hajj*,
                          pilgrimage.

Khalifah: see caliph.

Kitmann: to conceal.

Lawa: to twist (words).

Madrassa: a college whose primary function is the
                          teaching of law and related religious
                          subjects.

Maktab: elementary school for teaching chil-
                          dren recitation of the Qur'an and the
                          basis of reading and writing.

Mahdi: the directed one; a ruler to appear on
                          earth in the last days.

Mansukh: abrogated, annulled; a Qur'anic verse
                          or decree annulled or replaced by
                          another verse.

Manuscript: a hand-written record, from before
                          the invention of printing, which can
                          often be identified with a certain
                          period of history by the material on
                          which it is written and the style of
                          writing.

Masoretic text:	the basic text of the Old Testament, used for centuries in synagogues. It was produced by the Masoretes, a school of rabbis in Palestine and Babylonia in the eighth and ninth centuries CE. The word *Masorah* stands for explanation (Arabic: *Tafsir*).
Miraj:	lit. ladder, referring to the ascent of the Prophet to heaven in Jerusalem after the miraculous night journey.
Mufti:	an expounder of Islamic law.
Mufassir:	exegete; commentator.
Mushaf:	(pl. masahif), pages; manuscript; copy.
Nasikh:	a verse of the Qur'an which replaces an earlier verse from the same.
Naskh:	abrogation, the Islamic doctrine known as *al-Naskh wal-Mansukh*.
Papyrus:	vegetable product obtained mostly in the Nile valley; sheets made from the fibrous pith of the papyrus plant by pressing together two layers of strips at right angles to each other.
Parchment:	thin layers of animal hide rubbed with pumice in preparation for writing on.
Pbuh:	An abbreviation of 'Peace be upon him'.
Qadi:	judge who adjudicates disputes on the basis of Islamic law.
Qira:	recitation, *Qari* is one who recites (the Qur'an).
Recension:	revision and compilation.
Saj:	rhymed prose known as *Saj'*; this form was well known among the pre-Islamic poets of Arabia. Saj' has no consistent rhythmic or metrical pattern,

but shares with poetry the element of rhyme known as *fasila* (pl. *fawasil*) and it is that feature which we find in the Qur'an.

Septuagint: the Greek version of the Old Testament written by seventy (or seventy two) translators in the third century BCE, hence the name Septuagint.

Sharia: the path to be followed; Muslim law, the totality of the Islamic way of life.

Shia: Shi'ite sect regarding Ali, the son-in-law of Muhammad as direct lawful successor to Muhammad; known also as Alids.

Sunna: the trodden path, custom, the practice of the Prophet and the early community which becomes for all Muslims an authoritative example of the correct way to live an Islamic life.

Sunnis: those who accept the Sunna and the historic succession of Caliphs, as opposed to the Alids; the majority of the Muslim community are Sunnis.

Surah: (pl. *suwar*), written also as *sura;* a row or series, chapter, a group of Qur'anic verses collected in a single chapter.

Tafsir: commentary and interpretation, the exegesis of the Qur'an.

Tahrif: to corrupt; scriptural alteration or corruption; *tahrif bi'al lafz*, textual alteration; *tahrif bi'al ma'ni*, corruption in the meaning.

Tawhid: unity, oneness; the doctrine of the unity of God.

Torah: the first five books of the Old Testament part of the Bible.

Ummah: Islamic community.

Uncial: writing in upper case, letters usually without separation of words. Sometime called *Majuscule*, the oldest form of Greek manuscript.

Variant (reading): one of a range of available readings at a given point in time.

Version: translation; often used for the New Testament text in a language other than the Greek, for example, Old Syriac Version or English Authorised Version.

Wahy: revelation, other words like *Ilham* and *Kashf* are used in a lesser manner.

Wazir: minister.

Bibliography

Abbott, Nabiah, *The Rise of the North Arabic Script and its Koranic Development*, Chicago: University of Chicago Press (1939).

Abbott, Nabiah, *Studies in Arabic Literary Papyri, 2: Qur'anic Commentary and Tradition*, Chicago: University of Chicago (1967).

Abd al-Baqi, Muhammad Fu'ad, *Al-Mu'jam al-mufahras li-alfaz al-Qur'an al-karim*, Cairo: Dar al-Hadith, Jamia al-Azhar (1987).

Abd al-Baqi, Muhammad Fu'ad, (ed.) *Sunnan Ibn Maja* (2 vols) Beruit: Al-Maktabah Ilmiah (n.d.).

Abdel Haleem, Muhammad, *Understanding the Qur'an: Themes and Style*, London: I.B. Tauris (1999).

Abdul Haqq, Shaikh, *Madarij-e-Nabbuwat*, (Urdu trans.) part 2, Karachi: Madina Publishing (1976).

Abu Zahrah, Imam, *Islami Madhahib*, (Urdu trans.) Faisalabad: Malik Sons (1984).

Adams, C. J., Quran: the text and its history, in *Encylopedia of Religion*, Mircea Eliade (ed.) New York: Macmillan (1987).

Adelphi G. and Hahn E., *The Integrity of the Bible According to the Qur'an and Hadith*, Hyderabad (1977).

Ahmad, Abdullah Salamah, *The Sunni and Shia Perspective of the Holy Qur'an*, Jeddah: Abul-Qasim Publishing House (1992).

Ajijullah, Alhaj A. D., *The Essence of Faith in Islam*, Lahore: Islamic Publications (1978).

Ajijullah, Alhaj A. D., *The Myth of the Cross*, Lahore: Islamic Publications (1977).

Akbar, *Israel and the Prophecies of the Qur'an*, Cardiff: Siraj Publications (1971).

Aland, Kurt and Barbara, *The Text of the New Testament*, Grand Rapids: Eerdmans (1989).

Ansari, Bashir, *Bible main tahrif ke matni Saboot* (Urdu) Rochdale (1986).

Asad, Muhammad, *The Message of the Qur'an*, Gibraltar: Dar Al-Andalus (1980).

Ata ur-Rahim, *Jesus: A Prophet of Islam*, London: MWH London Publisher (1983).

Ata ur-Rahim, *The Gospel of Barnabas*, Karachi: Qur'an Council of Pakistan (1973).

Aziz-us-Samad, Ulfat, *A Comparative Study of Christianity and Islam*, Lahore: Sh. Muhammad Ashraf Publications (1983).

Baggil, H. M., *Christian-Muslim Dialogue*, Kuwait: Revival of Islamic Heritage Society (n.d.).

Baidhawi, *Commentarius in Coranum*, (ed. H.O. Fleischer), Leipzig: Verlag Vogel (1878).

Bashiruddin, Mahmood Ahmad, *Invitation to Ahmadiyyat*, London: Routledge & Kegan Paul (1961, 1980).

Bashiruddin, Mahmood Ahmad, *Introduction to the Study of the Holy Qur'an*, London Mosque (1985).

Bayard, Dodge (ed. trans.) *The Fihrist of al-Nadim* (2 vols.) New York: Columbia University (1970).

Beeston, A. F. L. (ed.) *Arabic Literature to the End of the Ummayad Period* (Cambridge: Cambridge University Press (1983).

Bell, William Y., *The Mutawakilli of Al-Suyuti*, Yale University Dissertation (1924).

Brockett, Adrian, The value of the Hafs and Warsh transmissions for the textual history of the Qur'an, in Rippin, Andrew (ed.) *Approaches to the History of the Interpretation of the Qur'an*, Oxford: Clarendon Press (1988).

Brown, Colin (ed.) *New International Dictionary of New Testament Theology*, Carlisle: Paternoster (1986).

Bruce, F. F., *The Canon of the Scriptures*, Glasgow: Chapter House (1988).

Bruce, F.F., *The New Testament Documents: Are they reliable?* Leicester: Inter Varsity Press (1992).

Bruce, F.F., *The Books and the Parchments,* London: Pickering and Inglis (1978).

Bruce, F.F., *The Spreading Flame,* London: Paternoster Press (1958).

Burton, John, *The Collection of the Qur'an,* Cambridge: Cambridge University Press (1979).

Burton John, *The Sources of Islamic Law: Islamic Theories of Abrogation,* Edinburgh: University Press (1990).

Burton John (ed. tr.): *Abu Ubaid al-Qasim b. Sallam, Kitab al-nasikh wa-l-mansukh,* Cambridge: E. J. W. Gibb Memorial Trust (1987).

Burq, Ghulam Jilani, *Do Islam,* (Urdu), Lahore: Sh. Ghulam Ali Publishers (n.d.).

Carsten Peter, Thiede, *The Jesus Papyrus,* London: Weidenfeld & Nicolson (1996).

Carsten Peter, Thiede, Contributor to *Jesus 2000,* London: Lions Publishing.

Carsten Peter, Thiede, *Rekindling the Word: In Search of Gospel Truth,* Pennsylvania (1995).

Darwaza, Muhammad Izzat, *Al-Qur'an al-Majid,* Sidon-Beruit (n.d.).

Dashti, Ali, *Twenty Three Years: A Study of the Prophetic Career of Mohammad,* London: George Allan & Unwin (1985).

Dawood, Abdu L-Ahad, *Muhammad in the Bible,* Doha: Presidency of Shariyah Courts and Religious Affairs (1980).

Deedat, Ahmad, *Is the Bible God's Word?* Birmingham: Islamic Propagation Centre (1986).

Denffer, Ahmad von, *Ulum al-Qur'an: An Introduction to the Science of the Qur'an,* Leicester: Islamic Foundation (1985).

Doi, Abdur Rahman, *Qur'an: An Introduction,* Lahore: Kazi Publications (1990).

Esposito, John (ed.) *The Oxford Encyclopaedia of the Modern Islamic World* (Vol. 1–4) Oxford University Press (1995).

Fazlur Rahman, *Islam,* London: University of Chicago Press (1979).

Gattje, Helmut, *The Qur'an and its Exegesis,* (English trans. & ed. Alford T. Welch) Oxford: Oneworld (1997).

Ghulam Ahmad, Mirza, *Chashma Masihi*, (English trans.), Rabwah: Tabshir Publications (1972).

Ghulam Ahmad, Mirza, *Tawzih Maram*, (English trans.), Rabwah: Tabshir Publications (1972).

Ghulam Ahmad, Mirza, *Jesus in India* (English trans.) London: Ahmadiyya Muslim Foreign Mission (1978).

Sarwar, Ghulam, *Islam for Younger People*, London: The Muslim Educational Trust (1994).

Sarwar, Ghulam, *Islam: Beliefs and Teachings*, London: The Muslim Educational Trust (1984).

Gibb, H.A.R and Kramers, J. H., *Shorter Encyclopaedia of Islam*, Leiden: E.J.Brill (1995).

Gilchrist, John, *The Qur'an: The Scriptures of Islam*, Mondeor: MERCA (1995).

Gilchrist, John, *Jam'al-Qur'an: The Codification of the Qur'an Text*, Benoni: Jesus to Muslims (1989).

Glasse, Cyril. *The Concise Encyclopaedia of Islam*, London: Stacey International (1989).

Haeri, Sh. Fadhlalla, *Man in Qur'an and the Meaning of the Furqan*, Texas: Zahra Publications (1982).

Haley, John W., *Alleged Discrepancies of the Bible*, Grand Rapids: Baker Book House (1981).

Hasan, Ahmad (ed. tr.) *Sunan Abu Dawud* (3 vols) Lahore: Sh. M. Ashraf Publishers (1988).

Hastings, James (ed.) *Dictionary of the Bible*, Edinburgh: T & T. Clark (1921).

Hughes, Thomas Patrick, *Dictionary of Islam*, Delhi: Cosmo Publications (1978).

Hussain, Jassim M., *The Occultation of the Twelfth Imam: A Historical Background*, London: Muhammadi Trust (1982).

Hussain, Kamil, *Al-Dhikr al-Hakim*, Cairo (1972).

Ibn Hazm, *Kitab al-fisal fil-milal wal-ihawa'wal-nihal* (2 vols.) Dar ul-jil, Beirut (1985).

Ibn Hisham, *Sira* (trans. Alfred Guilliam, *The Life of Muhammad*) Karachi: Oxford University Press (1955).

Ibn Sa'd, Abu Abd Allah Muhammad, *Kitab al-Tabaqat al-Kabir*, (trans. S.Moinul Haq), 2 Vols, Karachi: Pakistan Historical Society (1967, 1972).

Ibn Khaldun, *The Muqaddimah*, (trans. Franz Rosenthal, abridged and edited by N. Dawood) London: Routledge & Kegan Paul (1987).

Imam Ibn Kathir, Tafsir Ibn Kathir, 2 vols. (Urdu trs.), Lahore: Maktaba Tamir Insanyat.

Izzat, p. 4; Rahmatullah part I, pp. 18–19.

Jadid, Iskander, *The Infallibility of the Torah and the Gospel*, Basel: Centre for Young Adults (n.d).

Jafri, S., Husain M., *The Origins and Early Development of Shi'a Islam*, Beirut: Librairie du Liban (1990).

Jalil, Yusuf, *The Authenticity of Scriptures*, Al-Mushir, Rawalpindi: Christian Study Centre (1976).

Jeffery, Arthur, *Foreign Vocabulary of the Qur'an*, Baroda: Oriental Institute (1938).

Jeffery, Arthur, *Islam: Muhammad and His Religion*, New York: Bobbs-Merrill (1958).

Jeffery, Arthur, *The Qur'an as Scripture*, New York (1952).

Jeffery, Arthur, *Materials for the History of the text of the Qur'an*, in Ibn Dawud, *Kitab al-Masahif*, Leiden: E.J.Brill (1937).

Jeffery, Arthur, Progress in the study of the Qur'an text, *Muslim World*, Hartford Seminary (1935).

Josephus, *Works of Josephus*, (trans. William Whiston) Edinburgh: Thomas Nelson (1841).

Kamali, Muhammad Hashim, *Principles of Islamic Jurisprudence*, London: The Islamic Texts Society (1997).

Kamal-ud-Din, Khawaja, *The Sources of Christianity*, Lahore: Muslim Mission & Literary Trust (1973, 1924).

Keller, Werner, *The Bible as History*, New York: William Morrow (1964).

Kelly, J. N. D., *Early Christian Doctrines*, New York (1967).

Kelly, J. N. D., *Early Christian Creeds*, London: Longmans (1967).

Khalifa, Rashad, *Qur'an: The Final Testament*, (Authorised English Version, 1992).

Khan, Izzat and Abdullah, Abu, *Divine Revelations, The Muslims and the Bibles: A Clarification*, Burnley (1998).

Khan, Muhammad Muhsin (ed. tr.) *Sahih al-Bukhari* (9 vols) Ankara: Hilal (1978).

Khui, Abu al-Qasim ibn Ali Akbar, *Bayan fi Tafsir al-Qur'an*, The

Prolegomena of the Qur'an, (tr. Abdul Aziz Sachedina) Oxford: Oxford University Press (1998).

Khurshid Ahmad, Khurshid, *Hazrat Usman Ke Sarkari Khatoot* (Urdu) Lahore: Idarah Islamiat (n.d.).

Lester, Toby, What is the Qur'an? *The Atlantic Monthly Company*, **283,** Arizona, (Jan. 1999).

Lings, Martin and Safadi, Yasin Hamid, *The Qur'an*, London: British Library (1976).

Macdonald, Duncan B., *The Development of Muslim Theology, Jurisprudence and Constitutional Theory*, London: Darf Publishers (1902, 1985).

McDowell, Josh and Gilchrist, John, *The Islam Debate*, San Bernadino: Here's Life Publishers (1983).

McDowell, Josh, *Evidence that Demands a Verdict*, San Bernardino: Campus Crusade (1979).

McDowell, Josh, *More Evidence that Demands a Verdict*, San Bernardino: Campus Crusade (1975).

McDowell, Josh, *Answers to Tough Questions about the Christian Faith*.

Malik, Arfaque, A beam in their eyes, *The Straight Path*, June 1988, Birmingham: Ahl Al-Hadith (1988).

Masood, Steven, *Jesus and the Indian Messiah*, Oldham: Word of Life (1994).

Maurice, Bucaille, *The Bible, the Qur'an and Science*, (trans. Pannell and Bucaille), Paris: Seghers (1988).

Mawdudi, Abul A'ala, *Towards Understanding the Qur'an*, Vol 1, (ed. Zafar Ishaq) Leicester: Islamic Foundation (1988).

Mawdudi, Abul A'ala, *Tafhim ul-Qur'an*, (Urdu), Vol. 1, Lahore: Idara Islamiat (1973).

Mawdudi, Abul A'ala, *The Message of the Prophet's Seerat*, Kuwait: Islamic Book Publishers (1982).

Mendelsohn, Isaac, The Samarqand Kufic Qur'an, *Muslim World*, 30, Hartford Seminary (1940).

Mernissi, Fatimah, *Women and Islam: An Historical and Theological Enquiry*, Oxford: Blackwell (1995).

Metzger, Bruce M. and Coogan, Michael D., *The Oxford Companion to the Bible*, Oxford: Oxford University Press (1993).

Metzger, Bruce M., *The Text of the New Testament: Its Transmission, Corruption, and Restoration,* Oxford: Oxford University Press (1992).

Metzger, Bruce M., *The Canon of the New Testament: Its Origin, Development, and Significance,* Oxford: Clarendon Press (1997).

Naqvi, Qamar, *Sahayef* (Urdu) Lahore: Maqbool Academy (1983).

Nassr, Syed Hossein, *Responses to Hans Kung's paper on Christian Muslim Dialogue, The Muslim World,* **77,** Connecticut: Duncan Black Macdonald Centre (1987).

Nomani, Mohammad Manzoor, *Irani Inqilab* (Urdu) Lucknow: Al-Furqan Books (n.d.).

Nomani, Mohammad Manzoor, *Khomeini, Iranian Revolution and the Shi'ite Faith,* London: Furqan Publications (1988).

Pasha, Muhammad Abdulla, *Sixth Century and Beyond: The Prophet and his times,* London: Taha Publishers (1993).

Pfander, C.G., *Mizan ul Haqq: Balance of Truth,* London: The Religious Tract Society (n.d.).

Philips, Bilal, *The True Message of Jesus Christ,* Dar al-Fatah (1996).

Pickthall, Marmaduke Muhammad, *The Meaning of the Glorious Koran,* Delhi: Taj Company (1989).

Pickthall, Marmaduke Muhammad, *Holy Qur'an,* p.380.

Ragg, L. and L., *The Gospel of Barnabas,* Oxford: Clarendon Press (1907).

Rahim, Muhammad Ataur, *Jesus: A Prophet of Islam,* London: MWH Publishers (1983).

Rahimuddin, Muhammad, (Ed trans.) *Muwatta Imam Malik,* Lahore: Sh. Muhammad Asraf (1985).

Rahman, H. U., *A Chronology of Islamic History,* London: Taha Publishers (1995).

Rahmatullah Kairanvi, Muhammad, *Izharul Haqq,* (English) (3 vols) London: Taha Publishers (1990).

Rahmatullah, Kiranwi, *Bible say Qur'an Tak,* Izharul Haqq (Urdu) edited by M.Taqi Usmani), 3 Vols, Karachi: Darul Ulum (n.d.).

Rashid Rida, Muhammad, *Tafsir al-Qur'an al-hakim al-shahir bi-tafsir al-Manar* (12 vols) Beirut: Dar al-Ma'arif (n.d.).

Razi, Muhammad b. Umar al-Fakhr al-Din, *Al-Tafsir al-Kabir* (8 vols, Beirut: Dar al-Fikr (1978).

Rippin, Andrew and Kneppert, Jan (eds. tr.) *Textual Sources for the Study of Islam*, Manchester: Manchester University Press (1986).

Rippin, Andrew (ed.) *Approaches to the History of the Interpretation of the Qur'an*, Oxford: Clarendon Press (1988).

Robson, James (ed. tr.) *Mishkat al-Masabih* (2 vols) Lahore: Sh. Muhammad Asraf (1975).

Robinson, John A.T., *Redating the New Testament*, London: SCM Press (1984).

Robinson, Neal, *Discovering the Qur'an, A Contemporary Approach to a Veiled Text*, London: SCM Press (1996).

Sale, George, *Preliminary Discourse to the Koran*, London: Frederick Warne (n.d.).

Salih, Subhi, *Ulum al-Qur'an*, (Urdu tr. Ghulam Ahmad), Faisalabad: Malik Sons (1984).

Sell, Edward, *The Faith of Islam*, London: SPCK (1907).

Sell, Edward, *The Historical Development of the Qur'an*, Kent: People International (n.d.).

Shafaat, Ahmad, *The Question of Authenticity and Authority of the Bible*, Montreal: Nur Media Services (1982).

Siddiqi, Abdul Hamid (ed. tr.) *Sahih al-Muslim*, 4 vols, New Delhi: Kitab Bhawan (1982, 1984).

Siddiqi, Muhammad Zubayr, *Hadith Literature: Its Origin, Development and Special Features*, The Islamic Text Society (1991).

Slomp, J., The Gospel in Dispute, *Islamo Christiana*, **4**, Rome: Pontifico Instituito de studi Arabi (1978).

Sox, David, *The Gospel of Barnabas*, London: George Allen and Unwin (1984).

Suyuti, Jalaluddin, *Al-Itqan fi Ulum al-Qur'an* (2 vols.) (Urdu tr. Halim Ansari), Lahore: Idarah Islamiat (1982).

Tabari, Abu Jafar Muhammad b. Jarir, *The Commentary on the Qur'an*, (trans. J. Cooper), Vol.1, Oxford: Oxford University Press (1987).

Tabari, Abu Jaffar Muhammad b. Jarir, *Jami al-Bayan an Tawil al-Qur'an* (16 vols) Cairo: Dar al-Ma'arif (1955–69).

The New International Dictionary of Biblical Archaeology, p.294. Ed. 1983.

Tisdall, W. St. Clair, *Yanabiul Islam*, (Urdu), Lahore: Punjab Religious Book Society (n.d.).

Tisdall, W. St. Clair, *The Original Sources of the Qur'an*, London: SPCK (1924).

Vidyarthy, Abdul Haque, *Muhammad in World Scriptures*, 3 vols, Lahore Ahmadiyya Anjuman Isha'at Islam (1968).

Wansborough, John, *Quranic Studies: Sources and Methods of Scriptural Interpretation*, Oxford: Oxford University Press (1977).

Watt, William, M. and Bell, R., *Introduction to the Qur'an*, Edinburgh University Press (1991).

Welch, A. T. 'Al-KUR'AN' in *The Encyclopaedia of Islam*, 5: 400–432, Leiden: E.J. Brill (1990).

Williams, Derek. (ed.), *New Concise Bible Dictionary*, Leicester: Inter-Varsity Press (1989).

Woodbridge, John D. and Carson, D. A., *Scripture and Truth*, Carlisle: Paternoster Publishing (1995).

Yusuf Ali, Abdullah. *The Meaning of the Holy Qur'an*, Maryland: Amana Corporation (1983, 1989).

Yusuf Ali, Abdullah, *The Holy Qur'an: English Translation of the Meanings and Commentary*, Madinah: King Fahad Qur'an Complex (1410 AH).

Zafrullah Khan, *Islam: Its Meaning for Modern Man*, London: Routledge & Kegan (1980).

Zamakhshari, Mahmud b. Umar, *Al-Kashshaf*, 4 vols, Beirut: Dar al-Kitab (1947).

Zia'ai, Asi. *Barnabas ki Injil*, Lahore: Islamic Publications (1981).

Roots of Religion, Qum: Dar Rah-e-Haq (1982).

The Holy Qur'an with English Translation and Commentary, Vol. 1, Tilford: Islam International Publications (1988).

The Children's Book of Islam, Part One, Leicester: Islamic Foundation (1994).